boyzone

LIVING THE DREAM

EDDIE ROWLEY

EBURY
PRESS

First published in Great Britain in 1997

1 3 5 7 9 10 8 6 4 2

© 1997 Boyzone. Under licence to Underworld. Licensed by Copyright Promotions Limited.

Eddie Rowley has asserted his right to be identified as author of this Work.

Ebury Press
Random House, 20 Vauxhall Bridge Road, London SW1V 2SA

Random House Australia Pty Limited
20 Alfred Street, Milsons Point, Sydney, New South Wales 2061, Australia

Random House New Zealand Limited
18 Poland Road, Glenfield, Auckland 10, New Zealand

Random House South Africa (Pty) Limited
Endulini, 5A Jubilee Road, Parktown 2193, South Africa

Random House UK Limited Reg. No. 954009

A CIP catalogue record for this book is available from the British Library

ISBN 0 09 185416 4

Design by Blackjacks
Colour reproduction by Scanners
Photography by Philip Ollerenshaw
All photographs supplied by Idols Licensing and Publicity Ltd © 1997
Printed and bound in Portugal by Printer Portuguesa L.d.a.

Papers used by Ebury Press are natural, recyclable products
made from wood grown from sustainable forests.

INTRODUCTION

At the start of the year, we braced ourselves for a crazy ride through 1997. We knew it was going to be action packed all the way, and it has certainly lived up to our expectations. Here in the Boyzone camp, there was intense excitement as we embarked on a new chapter in the life of the band.

Four years down the road we've learned a lot, met all kinds of interesting people, been to some of the most stunningly beautiful parts of the world and achieved a level of fame that has allowed us to move several steps up the ladder on the pop scene. This year we pooled all our experiences to create a new live extravaganza that we're very proud of.

But it's not going to stop here. We plan to make our stage shows more and more exciting all the time. We know that you have to crawl before you walk, so we started off very low key, with basic live shows because that's all we could afford. But every year it has been building and building. Now we're co-writing and recording with the world's top producers on our new songs. And we enjoy thrills such as working with some of our favourite stars like Mr Bean (Rowan Atkinson), who featured in the video of our smash hit, 'Picture of You'.

In 'Living the Dream' we teamed up with our pop writer pal Eddie Rowley to take you inside the world you have created for Boyzone. We hope you enjoy your journey through this book as much as we have enjoyed our adventures as they happened. And it's all thanks to you, our wonderful fans. If it wasn't for your loyal support, Boyzone would still be just a dream for us. You are the life-blood of the grouip. We love you all.

RONAN KEATING

The two young men sipping drinks and huddled in conversation together in a corner of a Dublin club were attracting curious glances. Revellers out on the town did a double take.

Could it really be former Take That star Gary Barlow chatting animatedly with Ronan Keating, the current king of the boy-band brigade? It was. There they were, thick as thieves, sharing experiences of life in showbusiness and having a laugh.

The young guns of pop were developing a friendship that had ignited when they met up at pop icon Elton John's fiftieth birthday party. They were destined to become good mates. Ronan had always been described as the Gary Barlow of Boyzone. They are alike in many ways. Both are quiet and sensible. Gary was the main creative force in Take That. Ronan has been leading the way on that front in Boyzone. They both have a serious approach to their work and take pride in what they produce. And both are talented songwriters and singers. Ronan had made no secret of the fact that he was a big fan of Take That. He was in awe of the amazing success they achieved. And he openly admitted how he admired Gary Barlow.

Then it became Boyzone's turn to ride the dizzy heights of pop stardom. Gary Barlow looked on and he saw a mirror image of himself in Ronan. Gary says, 'I always thought that if I was ever to strike up a friendship with any of the guys in Boyzone, it would be with Ronan. I think I knew instinctively that we would get on very well together. Ronan has a quiet personality and I like quiet people. He's also a very talented

songwriter and singer and I admired him for that. I even suggested recording a duet together.'

It's his enormous charm and warmth as much as his talent that has seen Ronan climb the popularity stakes. And he has enjoyed the rewards ... and the awards. Ronan, along with Steve, went a step further than realising every young kid's dream of performing on the legendary UK pop show, *Top Of The Pops* – they also co-presented the weekly TV programme. It was another great moment for Ronan and he enjoyed every minute of it. Then there was the *Smash Hits* Poll-Winners' Party last year which saw him take the personal

awards for being the Most Fanciable Person, having the Best Haircut and being the Best Dressed in the business. He performed with Boyzone and Peter Andre on last year's MTV Music Awards extravaganza, which had an audience of 250 million. And then he capped it all this year by co-presenting the Eurovision Song Contest, as well as writing the interval song and performing it with the rest of the Boyz. Teaming up with the hilarious Mr Bean for 'A Picture Of You' was also a thrill ... the list is endless. Ronan is living a charmed life.

Elton John, George Michael and Gary Barlow are all superstars of pop who have spotted the star quality that Ronan possesses. But more than that, they have been won over by his courteous and genuinely friendly manner. He's been dubbed Mr Nice Guy and, although he is constantly under pressure after voluntarily taking on the role of Boyzone's leader, Ronan's perfect image has never been shattered. He's got a cool head on his young shoulders and he has fast learned how to cope with problems and difficult situations. Some people shout and scream when they're under pressure. Ronan holds his fire and tries to solve things in a reasonable fashion. He always makes an effort not to hurt other people's feelings. 'No, I never knock anybody,' he says. 'None of us in Boyzone has ever done that. It has never been in our nature to knock anybody. I think that's what gave Boyzone the good name we have. I'll give my opinion to anybody, but I'll never knock anybody in any way because I think that's terrible. Everybody tries their best to be something and it's not fair to knock them.'

Mention his Nice Guy tag and Ronan gets slightly embarrassed. 'I'm not perfect,' he says. 'I do get annoyed about things. Everybody does. That's human nature. I wouldn't be normal if I didn't. There are a lot of things to deal with in the group because so much is happening all the time and there are decisions to be taken.

'With so much going on problems do arise, but I prefer to sort them out without a row. If there's a problem I'll say it. I'll sit the person down and say. "OK. da.da.da. solve the problem now. Don't let it go any further." I don't like crap. I don't like stern stuff or anyone feeling bad or anyone backbiting. Sort it out now, that's it. I never see myself as Mr Nice Guy . I just am what I am. My mother and father brought me up to be me, to be what I am today. They told me never to lie and I don't. They've taught me to be honest with people and that's the way I am.

'I don't freak out when things go wrong. I'm not a violent person. I don't shout and scream. I do the old 'count to ten trick'. Calm down, here we go, sort it out logically. Everything can be solved, that's my theory. If there's a problem it can be solved without falling out with people or losing colleagues and friends. You've got to think about things before you act. Some people panic. A lot of people in this business, friends of mine, panic when they get into situations. They should think about the problem and work it out.'

When he's socializing in a crowd, Ronan doesn't hog the limelight. He doesn't seek to be the centre of attention. He prefers to be just one of the gang. In fact, he enjoys the company of people who are fun to be with, people who are entertaining in their own right. He'll sit back, enjoy their stories, gossip and jokes and have a laugh.

Ronan has literally grown up in showbusiness. He was only sixteen when he left school to join Boyzone. But he has no regrets about missing out on all the fun that goes with teenage years, like hanging out with friends, going clubbing and meeting girls. Ronan's feet haven't touched the ground since he was launched to stardom and his life has been racing by at the speed of light. One minute he was a boy with

dreams for the future. Now he's a young man living the dream. In between, a chunk of his childhood went missing.

He reflects: 'I've gained more than I've lost. I do admit I did lose a little bit of my childhood, but it's fine. I will live through that with my children, I hope, some day. I'm glad of where I am and I'm very proud of what I have achieved and of where we all are today, the five of us.

'I'm aware of the fact that I'm definitely a different person. Everybody grows up, and from the ages of sixteen to twenty-six, I think, is the most changing part of people's lives. I have changed an awful lot. My eyes have opened up to a lot of things and my mind has opened up to a lot of things. I've become more cautious of people. I've become a little bit harder. I was very soft when I joined the band. I was very sensitive and soft. I have toughened up an awful lot. People around me made made me tougher. I don't know if that's a good thing or a bad thing, but I have. I feel wiser. I feel more confident. I'm more streetwise and I have matured.'

As Boyzone's fame spread, it allowed Ronan – along withe the other Boyz – the opportunity to visit foreign destinations. That, too, has changed him. He says, 'Most people in Ireland live in their back gardens for most of their lives. Some of them never even get to go away at all or whatever. Or fly on a plane. I've been around the world. I don't think there is anywhere left to see for me, apart from the North Pole or somewhere like that. It has definitely opened my eyes and taught me how to treat people better. It has taught me about what actually goes on in the world outside my back garden. It's a wonderful world, wonderful – so many different cultures and races and wonderful people. And I've been able to experience all that thanks to the success of Boyzone. The fans, of course, have made it all possible. I'll never forget that. Never.'

The fans are waiting outside a hotel in the UK where Boyzone are staying. They're hoping to catch a glimpse of their idols going in and out. The Carter Twins, Stephen and Tony, arrive by taxi. Ronan is with them and all hell breaks loose as the young girls go into a frenzy and swarm around the car. Ronan is mobbed as he runs the gauntlet on his way into the hotel reception.

Whenever Ronan appears, the sight of him drives the girls wild. Just a glimpse of his blond head at a window and the deafening sound that erupts is like a bomb exploding. But he soaks it all up. And it's not just the fans who want a piece of him. Ronan is also the main focus of media attention. He's the one the journalists ask to interview. It all piles on the pressure as his work rate increases, but he seems to take it all in his stride. Ask how he copes and he'll tell you that he loves every minute of it. And when you're doing a job you love, you feel like you're never working a day in your life. 'What have I got to complain about?' he asks. 'I'm living every young guy's dream. I think to be in a pop band at this age is unbelievable. We get to travel around the world and meet some wonderful people. We have a couple of quid in our pockets. We get a chance to stand on stage in front of 13,000 people who're screaming for us. It is wonderful.

'I wouldn't know what to do if I woke up in the morning and discovered it was all gone. I wouldn't know what to do. I would be lost. I love it so much. I've built my life around this so much now. And everything I do revolves around this band. I love it so much I eat, sleep and drink Boyzone. It is everything that I'm about right now and everything I want to be about for as long as it can be. I love it with all my heart. I love taking the responsibility. I love writing the songs, singing the songs and doing the interviews. If I didn't enjoy it I wouldn't do it.'

Ask the most cynical people and they'll tell you they can't find any faults in Ronan, no matter how hard they try. He's honest and sincere and good friend to have on your side. And there's a deep side to him that makes Ronan all the more interesting: he's not your average fickle pop star. He's got a good grasp of life that comes from his religious upbringing.

Ronan is not embarrassed talk about his deeply held spiritual beliefs. 'I'm a very religious person,' he says. 'But I don't preach and I only talk about it when I'm asked in interviews. I'm not ashamed of what I am. I love God. I love the Lord so much. *He* has brought me to where I am today. *He* has kept me safe, strong and healthy. *He* has put everyone of us in this

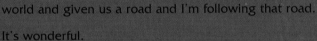

world and given us a road and I'm following that road. It's wonderful.

'It would be naive for me to think that the man upstairs isn't really there. My religion keeps me going. And it has kept my mother going through everything. I love the Lord.'

The leather-clad young man in black weaves through the Dublin traffic on his majestic motorbike. Like a knight in shining armour he roars up to the city's trendy Chocolate Bar, owned by his co-manager John Reynolds. Ronan has a new toy and he's proudly showing it off. It's the bike of his dreams, a Harley Davidson. A black Cherokee jeep is parked at the entrance to the POD nightclub. That's also Ronan's – not bad for a lad who dropped out of school at sixteen.

He says, 'Since I was a kid, I dreamed of owning a Harley Davidson and riding across America with the wind in my face. I'm halfway there. I've bought a Harley and it's fantastic. It's hard to describe the sensation you get when you're riding it. It's just one of the greatest thrills in the world. A horse or a motorbike ... it's the same.'

The Harley Davidson is a symbol of the success Ronan has achieved, but he has also had to make sacrifices. It hasn't been easy for him to have relationships because he's never in one country for long enough to hold down a serious romance. But there's time enough for all of that when Boyzone is over. It doesn't mean that there are no flirtations along the way. That's allowed.

He says: 'I've had a lot of girls that are friends. I've had a girlfriend while I was in the band, but nothing serious. I can't ... I couldn't. It wouldn't be fair on me or her. This is just a hectic pace of life and I'd never see her. It's easier not to get involved.

'Relationships are something you have to give a lot of time to and the emotional stress that would be involved in my case, because I'm never around, would be just too much to handle for either of us. That's just the way it is and I accept that because I have a long life ahead of me, so I won't miss out on anything in the long run. I'm content to have my personal life with my family and friends. They're still there for me and that's the main thing.'

Since Boyzone became known outside Ireland, Ronan has only had the opportunity to make rare visits to Dublin. But while he has been to some of the most exotic, breathtaking and heavenly places on the planet, he's still attracted to the Emerald Isle, as his native land is often referred to. 'Well, home is home. Home is where you are born and reared and brought up. It's where you know best. After Boyzone, God bless us, I'll travel around the world and I'm sure I'll live somewhere like America, the Far East or Australia for a time. But I think that eventually I'll come home to Dublin and settle down.'

HIGH FLYING

The moment you're told, 'The plane's going down,' is every jet-setter's nightmare.

Boyzone couldn't believe the nightmare was happening to them as they flew above the land of Oz, heading out into a wonderland to shoot their video for the single, 'Isn't It A Wonder'. The Fab Five were winding their way over the Australian desert at the midnight hour in mid-February 1997 when they were jolted out of sleep as their small twin-engined plane suddenly dropped 4000 feet.

Only thrillseeker Keith, sitting up front with the pilot and living out his dream, was instantly aware of the terrifying situation that began to unfold.The turbo on one of the engines had failed and Keith's heart skipped a beat as he listened through the earphones and heard the pilot request a full emergency landing at the nearest small airport in the remote wasteland. Ronan, Steve, Mikey and Shane were woken: the sudden drop in altitude had sent their ears popping.

Ronan says, 'It all happened so quickly that no one, apart from Keith, really knew what was going on. But the piercing pain in my ears told me that we had been through something. It was like someone had stuck a knife into them.'

It was only when their seven-seater plane suddenly went into an emergency landing procedure that they realized they were caught up in an air drama. The pilot allayed their fears and reassured the Boyz that the danger had passed. So the daredevils, who are speed freaks and love the thrills of car racing, were then able to enjoy the adrenaline rush from their sky antics.

After they landed at a remote airport in the middle of the desert, Ronan revealed how they interviewed each other on a video camera about the bizarre experience. 'It was worrying at first, but then it turned into a buzz ... a bit of a laugh. When we got off the plane we did a David Bellamy on it. We took out the camera and it was like, 'Well, here we are in the middle of nowhere. We didn't know where we were. We were stuck in the middle of the desert at midnight with a pilot we didn't know. It was weird.'

When they came to terms with the reality of the situation – that they could have been killed – the Boyz immediately phoned their mothers on their mobile phones to break the news and assure theire families that they were all safe and unhurt. Ronan says, 'We wanted to tell them ourselves and reassure them that we were OK, in case they learned of it through the media and feared the worst. And just as well, too, because there were a lot of sensational stories in the papers about the incident. It was completely blown out of proportion. They said that Mikey was so scared he'd never fly again. But nothing could be further from the truth. Sure, we all hopped on another plane immediately afterwards. I'm not saying we're macho, but it takes a lot to ruffle us.'

The air saga began after the turbo failed on one of the engines and the plane suddenly dropped from 8000 feet to 4000 feet in seconds. 'We could have continued on the journey,' says Ronan, 'but the pilot decided to land just in case.'

Mikey confesses, 'It was nerve-racking stuff at the time. The plane was all over the place coming in to land. We all tightened our seat belts and hoped for the best.

Buddy Holly [the American singer killed in a plane crash] was going through my mind for some reason. I did think about death afterwards. My immediate thought was for my little daughter Hannah. I didn't want to see her grow up without her dad.'

The plane landed safely at a small airport in the desert. Ronan remembers, 'We were stuck there for half an hour before cars arrived to meet us and take us to another airport an hour's drive away. There was a jet waiting for us there and it took us to our destination.'

Their record-company publicist Sharon Dunne from PolyGram, who was on the flight, says, 'The guys were great. They laughed off the whole incident and didn't think twice about getting back on another plane.' Sharon admits that the incident was 'a bit scary. It was only when we got off the plane we thought, 'Oh sweet Jesus.' It could have been a disaster, but it wasn't. We were lucky'.

When the drama passed, the Boyz' immediate concern was to make the onward journey to their hotel as quickly as possible to catch some shut-eye because an early-morning start was looming for their video shoot. Allison Maund, editor of *Boyzone* magazine, was already at their motel, having made the journey on a

different plane. She, along with the rest of the crew, had been alarmed to hear about the incident, but relieved that no one had been hurt.

She says, 'We were told everything was fine. By the time Boyzone arrived, it was just two o'clock in the morning and they were more bothered about the fact that they all needed haircuts before shooting started at six or seven in the morning. So they were all going to get about twenty minutes sleep and that's how it ended up. They all had their hair cut. Sharon and I did their ironing. It was like, "Plane drama is behind us...on to the job in hand."'

Photographer Philip Ollerenshaw says, 'The morning after the plane saga it was like, "We're all going on a summer holiday in this rickety old van" ... and there was a contest to see who could spot the first kangaroo.The Boyz were acting like they were on a real adventure and I thought

they'd all be tired because they'd been up all night.

'Ronan and Mikey were really excited about the fact that there were horses in the video. They were also in seventh heaven because they got the chance to drive cars, a Land Cruiser and a Harley Davidson motorbike. So the tiredness and the previous night's drama just got forgotten about very quickly.'

The settings for the video shoot were around a small town called Broken Hill. Broken Hill was really too civilized for the shoot, as they were looking for a more remote locality. So they ended up driving about half an hour out into the desert.

Allison recalls, 'It was an amazing place. The setting was spectacular. It was very hot...it felt like being in a sauna and there were loads of flies as well. Just flies everywhere. Even when you went to bed at night you could still hear them buzzing in your sleep. Everyone was wearing these stupid fly

nets which looked ridiculous, but they were essential to keep the flies off your face.

'The minute we arrived on the set the first morning, Keith and Mikey disappeared off into the desert with a Cadillac, which was used as part of the shoot. They got into trouble because the guy who actually loaned the video company the Cadillac wasn't happy about it being driven very far. And there was Keith and Mikey disappearing into this dust cloud in the distance! Everyone was chewing their fingernails until the mad-cap pair returned because the owner was quite grumpy.

'We were absolutely in the middle of nowhere. And it was beautiful because it was red dust for miles and miles and miles. The old couple who appear in the video had a funny owl museum which we visited there. It's their home and they have a little annexe on it where they've got this owl collection. The house has no roof because it burnt off in a fire a few years ago and they've never been able to afford to replace it. And because it never rains there it's been no bother really.

'What's so upsetting is that their house was featured quite heavily in the movie, *Priscilla, Queen Of The Desert*, and they were trying to live off the tourism that came from that. The Boyz recognized it...every set we went to they were going, "Oh do you remember that? Do you remember that? That was in this scene. That was in that scene." A lot of the locations were also in *Mad Max*.

'There were tourists around and the Boyz were attracting quite a lot of attention. The tourists may not have known who they were, but there was filming going on so they knew the Boyz were a bit special.'

Philip says, 'By the end of the afternoon all the locals were chatting to the lads. It was a bit like an outback party

with people drinking beer and having ice creams. I think that's what comes across about this band, that wherever they go they always like talking to normal, real people. Instead of just sitting in their room being pop stars, they like to get out and have fun with the extras on the set or the crew or whoever. They're often under tremendous pressure but I've never seen them really lose their cool and let it all go.'

The idea to use a Harley Davidson in the video was Keith's. With Ronan and Mikey on horses and Shane taking the wheel of the Chevrolet, Keith didn't want to be left out of the action. Steve isn't really bothered about being an action man. Philip says, 'Keith suggested using a Harley Davidson at nine o'clock in the morning and by 10am it had arrived. They managed to get the bike quite quickly – God knows where from. It was an afterthought. Keith didn't like the idea of just being a passenger in a car. He wanted to do something positive, something that looked visually interesting.

'I think he looks really good on the Harley. At first he didn't want to wear the helmet because he wanted to ride it with his hair flowing in the wind, but I think it was decided that he should wear it for safety reasons.

'They all come up with their own ideas for videos. They're very good at making an input. All of them. It's their job, but at the same time they spend so much time doing it that you need to be enjoying it. They get great satisfaction out of putting their stamp on things like videos. And as their

experience grows, their ability to make a valid contribution increases. Everyone thinks that Ronan is the main creative force, but they all chip in if they have an opinion.

'What other people think is also very important to them. They don't take it for granted that everything is going to work, everything is going to look great and they're always going to be fantastic. They talk to people, look for other views, ideas and opinions.

'Being in a band you have to compromise, and when you're together with the same bunch of people you learn what each other wants and a lot of the decisions are group decisions, although some individuals in the band are more assertive than others. A lot of people presume that bands have everything decided for them – not in this case at all. They're very interested in getting involved in every aspect of what they do.'

In 1997 Boyzone have had the opportunity to shoot videos in the most interesting and exotic locations, including Mexico as well as the Australian outback. They enjoyed a trip to the picturesque village of Cuernavaca, two hours from Mexico city on the road to Acapulco. That video was for the song 'Mystical Experience', which was released for fans in South America. You'll know it as 'Experiencia Religiosa', which was on the B-side of 'Isn't It A Wonder', and it was originally a massive South American hit for Enrique Iglesias, the son of famous Spanish crooner Julio Iglesias.

Mikey says: 'When we go to work in places like Cuernavaca it's an incredible feeling for us. Being plucked from an ordinary life in Dublin and ending up in such wonderful, far-away place like that ... it's just like a dream. We spent two days working on the 'Mystical Experience' video, which was shot in a big old hacienda [a large ranch with a house on it]. A great experience to look back on.'

Boyzone magazine editor Allison says, 'Cuernavaca had something very special about it. It was just really peaceful. It was out of the way and the weather was gorgeous. The video was done in a very laid-back style. It meant there was an hour between takes.

'The boys took full advantage of their free time by doing things like sunbathing, exploring and playing football. They burst one ball and had to get another one. Then they nearly destroyed a flying ants' nest in the eves of one of the ruined buildings on the hacienda. Then in the evening we had a bit of a sing-song and it was like guide camp. We were having our dinner and it was dark and we had all these candles lit and the Boyz and crew were singing all these ridiculous songs ... Abba songs and songs from *Grease*. It was like being on summer camp or something.'

It was also a dream location for their photographer Philip Ollerenshaw and he was very snap happy during the Boyz two-day sojourn in Cuernavaca. 'The Boyz have their photographs taken night and day and they must hate every minute of it. So, when you have a pop star come up to you and want you to take pictures, then you know you're in an interesting place. Any spare minute they had when they were shooting the video, they were coming up to me and wanting me to take pictures of them.'

MIKEY GRAHAM

*Wide-eyed Mikey Graham almost choked
on his sausage. The star with the smouldering
good looks blinked and did a double take.*

Sitting across from him in the dining-room of a smart London hotel at breakfast was one of his all-time heroes, Robert de Niro. Mikey's pulse raced and heart beat faster in a whirl of emotions as he grappled with the dilemma of whether or not to approach his idol. His mind was in a spin and his body throbbing with excitement – feelings that Boyzone fans around the globe can identify with. That's exactly how they react when they get to meet their heart-throbs in the flesh.

At that moment, Mikey was the fan. And he was determined not to let the opportunity pass without having a brief word with de Niro. But, conscious of the fact that not all celebrities enjoy the attention of fans, especially in private situations when they're having a meal, Mikey approached de Niro with caution. Like a tiger stalking its prey, he held off until the opportune moment presented itself when de Niro finished his food.

Sucking in a deep breath as he composed himself, Mikey rose from his chair and strolled over to De Niro. The legendary *Godfather* actor shot him with a stern look. Mikey's words were brief and direct. 'Excuse me,' he said. 'I just want to say hello to you, I'm a big fan.' Mr de Niro smiled and his response was courteous. 'Thank you,' he replied.

The Boyzone star turned away and strolled back to the other members of the group, glowing from the experience of having been in the presence of what he perceived to be greatness. But there was more to come. Mikey, Keith, Shane, Steve and Ronan were being interviewed by a gang of media people from around Europe that same morning. When Robert de Niro saw all the fuss around the Boyz, he was curious. Until then, he hadn't heard of Boyzone. But like the Godfather, he made some enquiries. And when he discovered that they were chart-topping popsters, de Niro went over to *their* table to say hello.

Mikey says, 'He told us that he hadn't heard of Boyzone and we weren't surprised because we weren't known in America. But he seemed genuinely interested in the group and he promised he'd look out for us in the future. Then he posed for a picture with us.'

It was a magic encounter that made Mikey Graham's day. Life in Boyzone is full of surprises and its one of the reasons that makes Mikey realize he's the luckiest guy in the world. He says, 'Meeting Robert de Niro was a very special moment for me. He's always been a hero of mine in the acting business and I was delighted to find that he's a warm, gentle kind of man. Not at all like the characters he portrays in the movies.

'He's a very interesting man. He has a very tough, strong image. The tough exterior is probably something that he has built up along the line. It's a sort of self-protection. It's an image that commands respect from people without him using a lot of words – without speaking, even. I don't want to sound conceited, but there's something about Robert de Niro that I can relate to.'

Mikey's own reputation is not unlike that of his idol. He has an appearance that gives the impression he's a hard man. The stern facial expression that could easily earn him the role of a Mafia henchman in a de Niro movie. Shane describes it as 'a funny frowny head on him'. It's only when fans meet Mikey in the flesh that they realise he's a warm, friendly guy with a

heart of gold. He'll willingly pose for photographs and autographs at Boyzone concerts, and he'll chat for ages if he's allowed. But Mikey is painfully aware that his visage – it's also been said he looks like moody actor Sean Penn – sometimes sends out the wrong signals to Boyzone fans.

He says: 'I know the way I look puts people off, but there's not a lot I can do to change that – unless I do a Michael Jackson and have cosmetic surgery. And I'd never go down that road. I don't throw myself all over people and maybe that's why some of them think I'm hard to approach. Robert De Niro is the only person I was ever in awe of, but I didn't let it show. I still played it very straight with him. I think he respected that as well.

'A lot of people in the entertainment business are shallow. They put on an act. If I'm at a showbiz party I'll spend time speaking to people who I consider to be real people. It's really up to other people to judge the type of personality I have. For my own part, I think I've got a split personality. I love what I do in Boyzone, being on stage, out in the public spotlight. I love all that. And I consider myself to be a very friendly person. But there's also another side to me. There's the off-stage person who's quiet, shy and retiring.'

Mikey has had his doubts about sticking the pace in Boyzone on several occasions, but they were just fleeting moments of madness. He says, 'Everyone hits a weak period. You wake up and you wonder if you can face another day because you no longer have any time for yourself. We really didn't have very much time off during the first couple of years and it took its toll on everyone. But at the end of the day, when you're honest with yourself, you know that this is the best life ever.

'Boyzone has given me a wonderful opportunity in this world. And at an early stage I made a conscious decision that I was going to enjoy every moment of it. I wasn't going to let it all pass me by and then look back on it. I want to live it while it's happening.'

Tag someone with the words 'pop star' and we turn to jelly when they come into our company. There are some performers who exploit this and live the role of Someone Special. They develop an attitude, don dark shades and surround themselves with burly bodyguards.

Like the other Boyz, Mikey has remained true to himself. But he does admit to enjoying all the attention that's generously lavished on Boyzone. He realizes it's a high-rolling, excitement-fuelled period in his young life that he'll probably never again experience. So he's going to savour every moment of it. He says: 'I'd be lying if I said I didn't enjoy the fuss and the attention around Boyzone when we're out in the public domain. I wouldn't be human if I didn't. But I also have a realistic approach to it. I know that if I wasn't in Boyzone people probably wouldn't give me a second glance. That's the reality of life and that's why I don't let all this stardom business go to my head. I'll enjoy it, but I won't allow it to mess me up.

'Doors open for you when you're a pop star. You're invited to all kinds of strange places and events that you would be excluded from if you didn't find fame. It's all a bit false, really. But it's still an experience not to be missed when the opportunity is presented to you. You'd be mad to miss out on all the chances that come your way.

'We work very hard in Boyzone. I don't think anyone can really appreciate the workload that we get through. There is no way you can explain the stress involved. It's very, very strenuous. There have been periods when it brought me to my knees. I try to pick myself up all the time and carry on. You have to keep on going and keep on smiling. So I'm sure we can be forgiven for enjoying the star treatment when it happens. It's great to walk into a room at some occasion and be greeted with a certain amount of respect. It's great to be part of that. It's in circumstances like that you can see how all your hard work has paid off. It's brilliant. It's a good feeling.'

As the oldest member of Boyzone, Mikey Graham admits he's conscious of the age gap. He stands apart from his pop pals in many areas. He doesn't share the same interest in clothes as the other Boyz. Mikey's passion for style has long since passed. He went through his obsession with the hot fashion of the day before Boyzone became a household name. He says, 'I'm less fashion conscious than the rest of the lads and, yes, it's probably because I'm the oldest member of the group. I went through that whole clothes phase between the ages of sixteen and nineteen and then the novelty wore off. Now it's hard to be forced back in time, forced to get back into all that clothes thing again.'

Recalling his first memory of meeting Mikey, Shane Lynch says, 'The first time I saw him he had this leather hat on and a red bandana and he looked really smooth. I thought he was pretty cool.' These days, Mikey says he only makes the effort to look 'pretty cool' when he's in the public eye. Away from the spotlight and the stage, he doesn't really think about it. He's a casual dresser when the Boyzone machine is switched off, wearing whatever is comfortable.

Nevertheless, Mikey reckons that he's got good personal taste. He knows what he wants and won't be swayed by what the advertisers and magazines promote. And unlike some of pop's biggest names, Mikey is not a designer-label victim. In fact, he has an aversion to that whole fashion genre. He says, 'I've never been a designer-label freak. Just because there's a certain brand on clothes doesn't make them more cool, trendy or special. In fact, some of of that gear is so weird and grotesque I wouldn't even sleep next to the bleedin' stuff, never mind wear it. I think it's attention seeking if you feel you have to wear that kind of gear.

'If Boyzone's stylist Alex wants me to wear something or to get a new hairstyle, I'll certainly be open to any suggestions he makes. I'm always conscious about keeping in line with the Boyzone image, but at the end of the day I'm my own man and I decide how I look and what I'm prepared to wear. There's never been a problem yet.'

If there's a downside to life in a pop group, it's the fact that you lose your private life and you rarely get to see your family and friends. That's difficult enough when you're single without commitments. But, as in Mikey's case, when you've got a girlfriend and a little daughter it can be torture at times. It's been a struggle for Mikey and Sharon to keep their relationship going while being separated for long periods due to his tours with Boyzone. And Mikey's enforced parting from his gorgeous little daughter Hannah has been a nightmare he's had to deal with.

Mikey says: 'I've had to put my normal life on hold – every little piece of it – because my career in Boyzone is so manic. It's been really tough with me being a dad and having to leave little Hannah behind to go off with the group. But if I didn't do this I wouldn't be able to support my child.

'It's been really tough to cope with Hannah treating me like a stranger after I've been away for a long time. Because she's only in her second year, I'm like a visitor in the house to her when I return home. That's a hurtful feeling. It takes a little time for her to warm to me. But I'm confident the personal side of my life will get better when all this slows down.

'Sharon and I have had our problems and the media getting involved doesn't help. Every relationship goes through bad patches, but we have the added pressure of the media focusing on us. I know the media have a job to do and personal feelings don't enter into it. It's a dog eat dog thing in that business. They will do good things and bad. You have to respect that, no matter how hard it is at times. Sharon and I are both optimistic about the future. You have to hold on tight.'

Success has brought Mikey financial rewards beyond his wildest expectations, but he uses his money wisely. 'I haven't been extravagant,' he says. 'I've a nice car [a gleaming black BMW]. All I want out of life is a nice house, a nice car and to go on a couple of holidays a year.

'I come from a family of seven. We had what we needed, but it was tough on my parents to support seven children. Luckily I've been able to repay them by buying them

nice things and making sure that they have no money worries. They want for nothing now. My dad is a retired carpenter and lives life to the full. He's always been a rock of strength. If he ever had anything bothering him we'd never know about it. He's happy that one of his children has excelled so much and all of his children have done well. He's a great man, my father. And, of course, behind every great man is a great woman and that's my mother.

'It'll be strange to go back to my normal life when all this is over. I'll be going back and trying to pick up from where I was in '93. That will be a rediscovering journey for Mikey Graham. I know it will be all very different. My friends will be very busy with their own lives. They'll probably be all married.

'I still have the group of friends I always hung out with. Their attitude to me hasn't changed nor has mine to them. Shane Murray is probably my closest friend and the rest of the group who're close are Gavin Doyle, Ann Maria Cushen and Darren Higgins.'

Mikey will stay in the music industry in the future, if he can realize the many ambitions that are being hatched in his brain and stored for the right moment. 'I have a lot of dreams in my head. I have a lot of visions that I've put on hold,' he says.

'There's something new and interesting that each one of us possesses underneath our role in Boyzone. I believe I have a lot more to offer. I play the guitar. I write songs. It's an older, deeper type of music. It's the basis for a solo career in the future when our run comes to an end. Hopefully, that won't be for a long time yet. I'm enjoying this too much right now for it to end.'

EUROVISION

'Oh, Jeezus. Oh, Jeezus.' The two teenage girls, dressed in school uniforms, looked like they were going to collapse in a state of shock.

'Oh, Jeezus,' they exclaimed in unison again as Ronan whizzed past them like a gust of wind on one of Dublin's side streets. The shocked young fans couldn't believe that they had come face to face with their pop idol. He had suddenly turned the corner, taking them completely by surprise. They were so stunned, they didn't even think to ask for his autograph. He was gone in a flash.

It was the week of the Eurovision Song Contest and the Boyz were back in their home city. Ronan was co-hosting the spectacular TV song contest, which is seen by 300 million people around Europe, and Boyzone were performing a special song during the interval centrepiece.

It's Europe's biggest song festival and the Boyz were thrilled to be playing leading roles in it. Ronan, in particular, looked like the cat who'd got the cream. The boy just couldn't stop smiling all week. He had grown up watching the Eurovision on the telly every year, never dreaming that he would one day be presenting it, never mind performing as a special guest. Ronan also co-wrote the interval song, 'Let The Message Run Free', with Boyzone's producer Ray Hedges. Life couldn't have been more exciting for him that week.

There had been a couple of hectic months leading up to the contest as the plans were drawn up for the super show. Ronan was chosen to present it after he appeared on the Irish TV chat show, the *Late Late Show*. He wasn't aware of it then, but he was being secretly auditioned by Noel

Curran, the executive producer of Eurovision. Ronan charmed the audience and TV viewers with his personable manner that night. Curran had also watched Ronan co-presenting *Top Of The Pops.* It left him in no doubt that Ro was the perfect choice for Eurovision.

Boyzone were also selected as the interval act. There was only one problem. They needed a special song. Once again, Ronan weaved his magic to save the day. He went off to the studio with the Boyz' producer Ray Hedges and emerged with an anthem called, 'Let The Message Run Free'. As fans know, it's on the B-side of their smash hit, 'Picture Of You'.

Ronan revealed: 'There were tracks coming in from different people and they weren't working out. So I said, 'If you give me a couple of days in the studio, I'll give you the

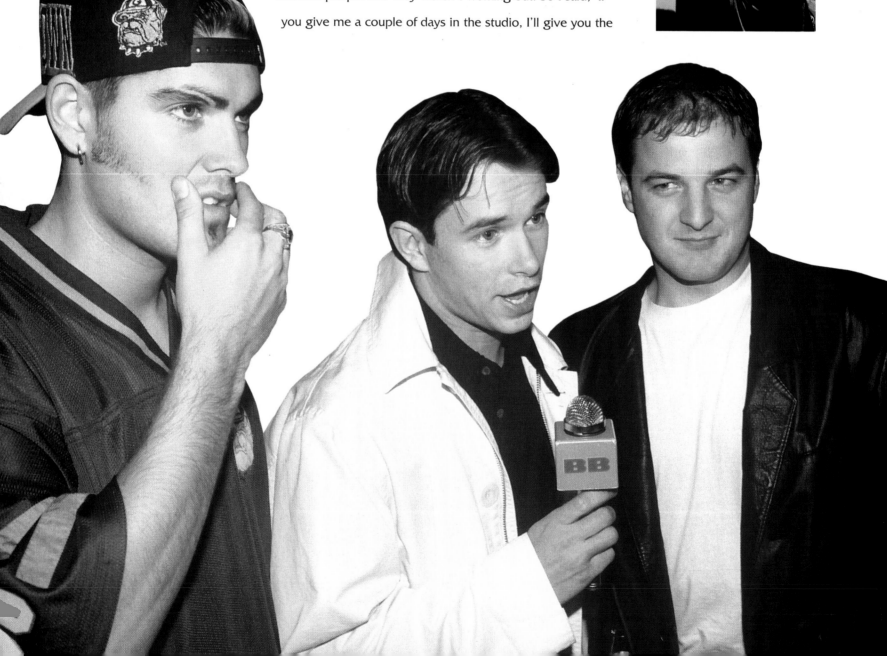

RONAN WITH FORMER IRISH P.M. JOHN BRUTON

for Ronan and the Boyz. They were trying to deal with Boyzone's commitments in Germany while preparing for Eurovision at the same time. The Boyz had to do intensive rehearsals in Dublin for their showpiece and Ronan was busy learning his role as co-presenter. With all the media from every European country in town, Ro was also in demand for interviews. But he still found time to party and even did some dare-devil driving around the local motor-racing track at Mondello Park. There was an anxious moment when he crashed his Fiat Uno, but he escaped without a scratch.

Ronan says, 'It was a very mad week for me, but to be honest, I was on such a high at the thought that I was hosting the Eurovision I didn't even think about the hard work involved. I had such a good time. I was the cream of the crop for that week.'

song.' They did and I spent a good few days in the studio with Ray. We had the brief, we knew what they wanted – a song with a communication theme in it. And we had an idea about what we needed as a record, what would be best for Boyzone and we built it. We knew exactly where we were going and we built it and it was a mountain of a song, it was huge. They wanted a cross between "Melting Pot" and "A Different Beat" and that's what they got.

'Noel Curran was delighted. He said, 'Thank God, this is what we're looking for.' I said, "There you go. I told you if you'd just give me the time, I'd give it to you. Give you the product." I love music. I love creating a song, sitting in the studio and building a song. With the Eurovision it was unbelievable, just building those tracks.'

The week of the contest, which was at Dublin's Point Theatre on Saturday, 3 May 1997, was also a frenzied time

AND WITH EUROVISION WINNER KATRINA

Ronan is at ease performing on stage, but presenting a TV spectacular was a new experience for him. Fortunately, he had the support of co-host Carrie Crowley, who works on Irish radio and TV. 'It was very different,' he says. 'I was co-presenting the biggest music television show in the world, which was nerve-racking when you think of it that way. But I felt very relaxed. Carrie was very easy to work with. We went through script rehearsals, but at the end of the day I wanted to do it as natural as I could. That's what I did. I was just relaxed as I could be. I enjoyed myself and had a laugh.'

Boyzone fans kept a vigil all week outside the the Point Depot where the Eurovision was staged. Security was tight because there had been a bomb threat and Steve got caught up in drama. One day he had problems getting into the venue because he didn't have a proper security pass. Even pleas of, 'But I'm performing in Eurovision with Boyzone,' fell on deaf ears. Then on another day, the taxi taking Steve to the venue wasn't allowed to take the star up to the gates due to security restrictions. Steve had to walk the rest of the way, and ended up under siege from fans.

Steve says, 'I told the policeman I was very late for rehearsals. "I need to be there, please can you let me up to the venue?" I pleaded. But he said, No.' So I had to get out and walk up and I warned the policeman that it was going to cause problems with so many fans around. Within seconds there were a load of girls on top of me, so the police officer had to come over and rescue me.'

It was also a special week for Mikey. He got the chance to be at home for his little daughter Hannah's first birthday party.

At the official press conference during Eurovision week, the Boyz told how proud they were to be involved in the TV extravaganza.

Said Ronan, 'We are ambassadors for our country when it comes to something as great as this.'

Keith added, 'It's a very proud feeling to be involved in something very, very important in our home country and home town.'

Mikey said, 'I think we will gain more credibility by appearing in Eurovision. It's great exposure for us.'

And back to Ronan, who said, 'My first memory of Eurovision is sitting in front of the TV with a cup of tea, watching Johnny Logan singing "What's Another Year" in 1980.'

UK EURO BOSS JONATHAN KING

It's a weird old world. Back then, Louis Walsh was Johnny Logan's manager. Johnny represented Ireland in the Eurovision that year and won the contest. Today, Louis is Boyzone's manager, the guru who created the pop supergroup and steered them to stardom. Louis had been involved in a hat trick of Eurovision victories. Logan won it twice, and his other protégée Linda Martin also captured the coveted crown. But the 1997 event was a special night for Louis as he watched his latest act take centre stage.

Choreographer Melinda McKenna built a mini-show around the Boyz for Eurovision. 'The song was about communication and unity, so we pulled in a lot of European dancers to create a show of unity in Europe,' Melinda said. 'We had dancers from Yugoslavia, Greece, Switzerland, Italy, a Scottish lady and three lovely Irish ladies. I'd been in Malaysia the year before and had seen a lot of people doing t'ai chi and found it absolutely stunning to watch and some of the movement came from that. They go into a sort of trance when they do it. It's almost like a meditation.

I have always wanted to do it in a show and that song was so right for it.

'There were fifteen dancers in total. I was working with the dancers while the Boyz were on tour in Germany. I did two days of rehearsals in London and then we all went over to Dublin. We worked in Dublin because we had the set, the scaffolding that we needed to work with, and then the Boyz came in for a couple of days and basically by the end of a week we had it in place. The directors of Eurovision looked at it and liked it. Then we had a ten-day period where we all went our separate ways and then came back together again for the last period. We rehearsed in greater depth in Dublin with the cameras, so we could check camera angles. It was an awful lot of work.'

Finally the big night arrived, and the Boyz had their mums and dads in the audience. It was a proud moment for their parents. Eurovision had always been a big event in their lives and now their sons were starring in it. And the President of Ireland, Mary Robinson, was in the auditorium watching them.

Keith recalls the moment: 'I've never felt so proud in my whole life. I always dreamt of playing in an All-Ireland Football Final at Croke Park [Ireland's national sports stadium] with the President there. That never happened for me, but the Eurovision has totally blown that one out of the water. It was just mind-blowing. There were tears in my eyes on stage.'

Steve adds: 'I remember some years ago looking at the Eurovision when Linda Martin was representing Ireland and I was thinking how I would love to be in the audience. So it was an unbelievable feeling to be actually performing in it.' Backstage as the countdown to the show began, Ronan was

busy autographing Eurovision programmes for the fans. He was totally relaxed.

Then it was his moment of glory as he stepped out on stage with Carrie Crowley to welcome 300 million viewers around Europe. The glint in his eye said it all. Ronan was in heaven. A new world-class TV presenter was born that night, and on top of that, Boyzone's performance was a dazzling affair. Later, Ronan treated himself to some champagne as the votes came in from countries all around Europe.

And it was a giddy Boyzone star who escorted the UK winner, Katrina, back on stage. The party continued into the early hours of Sunday morning. But there was no sleep for Boyzone.

They were back on a plane at 7 am to Italy for a TV show. Eurovision was another chapter in their amazing career. But the Boyzone show continued. Ronan added: 'I have to say, presenting and performing in Eurovision was the greatest moment of my life. I'd love to do it all over again.'

STEVE GATELY

His wall-to-wall smile lights up the concert venue.
Stephen Gately is the happiest man in the world.

The young star is in his favourite place on earth, out in the spotlight, centre stage, performing one of his own songs. Steve is the enigmatic one in Boyzone. He's quiet. Always deep in thought. A bit of a loner. There is only one person who really knows the real Steve Gately ... and that's Steve Gately himself. He surrounds his innermost thoughts and feelings with a shroud of secrecy.

While you'll often find the other Boyz larking about backstage at shows, Steve won't be part of the carry on. He's not interested in action-style games that the lads dream up to pass the time. He remains aloof, seemingly contented to enjoy his own company. He'll slip away to write a song or do some shopping. But plant Steve out in the spotlight and he opens like a flower in the sunshine. His gargantuan smile says it all. The stage is one of the things that makes life worth living for Steve. It gives him a buzz, an adrenaline rush that charges his whole being and makes him come alive. Watching Steve perform, you can see him being transformed before your eyes. Backstage he's friendly but subdued. He disappears, then emerges again from nowhere like a ghostly figure. And when he's in a room you hardly even notice him because he's such a silent person.

Always immersed in his own little world, Steve gives the impression of being troubled sometimes. And he does admit that, despite his enormous talent and incredible success, he still lacks a lot of self-esteem. He finds it difficult to accept that he's a heart-throb to millions of adoring fans all around the world. It's not that he's unhappy with his lot. Steve is very conscious of the wonderful life that Boyzone has opened up for him. He's had his dreams fulfilled and every month and each new year brings fresh opportunities into his amazing world. Steve enjoys his life as a pop star. But he's very hard on himself.

He says, 'To be honest, I had a lot more confidence at the start. Personally, I do think I had more at the beginning of Boyzone than I have now. I think my self-assurance has dropped a bit. I mean, I still have an extremely high confidence level when I'm on stage. That's the only place I've ever really had my confidence, up on the stage. It's still there. Everytime I am on the stage my confidence is there, no matter what. That's never changed, but the confidence in myself as a person has changed. It has dropped. I don't have as high an opinion of myself as I used to. I don't know why that is, but my self-esteem isn't what it should be.'

All the awards that Boyzone have achieved haven't served to boost Steve's personal opinion of himself. No amount of tributes in the magazines have made a difference to him. 'It has nothing to do with the achievements,' he says. 'I can't really explain it. I think it's just ... it's just something that happened really. My confidence just faded away. I wake up and I don't see myself as being anything special,

not that I ever did really see myself as being amazing looking or even a good looking person or anything like that. When I wake up in the morning it's like, "Oh God, another day." I try to make myself look half-decent and do my work.'

The fans will obviously be surprised by this admission. Usually when you achieve success in life, you gain a certain amount of attitude and confidence. And with the type of success that Steve has notched up, he should be strutting around like a proud peacock. To a degree, he says, Boyzone's chart-topping run in the pop world has helped to develop his personality.

'It has given me more confidence to talk to people,' Steve admits. 'I now have the confidence to talk to anybody. Before the band, I didn't. Now I can sit down and have a chat with anybody. But I'm not able to do things like, say, stand up for myself in situations. Like when I'm in the studio, things like that, I just find I can't stand up and say, "I want this and this." I can't seem to find the confidence to say that.'

On the positive side, Steve's humility is probably one of his endearing qualities. The fans and everyone around him respect Steve all the more because of his modesty. He doesn't possess a big ego and never will. It's not in his nature. But he's happy being Steve. 'I consider myself really lucky

to be given the opportunity that I've been given, knowing there are a lot of people out there who could have done the same as me, probably done it even better,' he says. 'I thank God so much.'

Like Ronan, Steve is deeply religious. It's his rock in life. He turns to the Lord during good times and bad. It helps him to keep his sanity, knowing that life is worth living and that there are even greater things ahead in the next world. Steve finds comfort in his religion and it brings peace into his life whenever the demands of being a pop star get too much for him. He says: 'I'll often go into a church just to relax and have a few quiet moments to myself. They are really calming places. Most times when I am at home in Dublin I go into Whitefriar Street church. That's near our record company, PolyGram. And, like I said in the past, it was there that I spent a lot of time praying to God that I would be chosen for Boyzone after I first did the audition to join the band. My prayers were answered and I've always gone back there to thank Him. If I am in that area I will always go into that church and put some money into the box for the poor and sit down and say a prayer for them. If I wasn't in the band I wouldn't have the ability to be able to do that and give money to people who are in need, the sick or the homeless. It's just a little way for me to say thanks.'

Steve doesn't openly flaunt his spiritual side. He says: 'I don't wear any holy things, although my mother has bought me a miraculous medal because I've been praying to Mary for a lot of reasons recently. I told my mother how I was praying. She said she would get me a miraculous medal 'cause she wears one. So I now wear that ... it protects me. But I don't flash it like some kind of badge.

'I have strong beliefs, but I don't try to shove them down other people's throats. I have nothing against other people having their own beliefs. I mean, if a person believes in something different that's their belief and that's not a problem. If somebody else has a different religion, I don't see that as a problem. I see a person who has their own mind to believe what they want to believe.

'My own religion has helped me cope with my life. When you pray to somebody, you're hoping somebody is listening and that somebody is going to answer your prayer. It's nice. And a church is just most amazing place. The quietness in a church is just unbelievable. I have to say I do like churches, I do like them.'

Steve's busy lifestyle on the road doesn't allow him the time to attend Mass every Sunday. 'It's something I haven't been able to devote my time to. I would like to. I would like to be able to go to Mass every Sunday, but I can't. My mum goes and she prays a lot for me. A lot of other people pray for me and they have a Mass dedicated to me. My name is read out in Mass. It's very touching. A person actually gets a Mass said for you. It's lovely. It's people who are praying that things are going to be all right and that you will continue to do well. They also pray to thank God that I am doing so well.'

Steve is doing well. His lifestyle is the stuff of dreams. But there's a lot of hard work involved. Life in a boy band demands a lot of commitment, make no mistake about it. It's a never-ending cycle of work that takes over your whole life. But there's no denying it is glamorous and fun.

He says, 'I do enjoy it. I enjoy the whole buzz of it. Being on stage, being in the studio, meeting people, getting to travel the world. I've just met so many people and done so many things. I have succeeded in doing a lot of things that I wanted to do. I'm enjoying myself.

'Boyzone has given me opportunities that I never dreamed of. If I hadn't been in this group, my life would have been so, so different. None of us expected the band to become so big. We hoped to do well, but we never imagined going to half the places we've been to. It's just wonderful. I am very, very thankful and grateful to the fans for that. I'm never, ever not nice to anyone. It's people who have made us what we are today. I believe in being nice to people. It's not a falseness. It's just the way I am really.

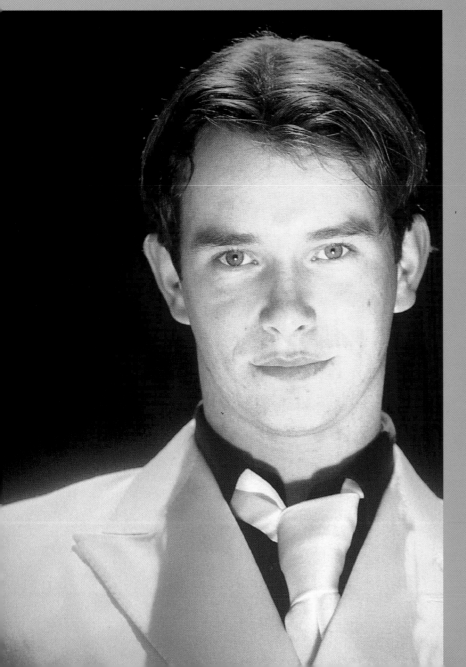

'It's not all glamorous, of course. A lot of people only see the glamour and the glitz. They think it's amazing hotels and limousines here, there and everywhere. It's not like that. It's a tough job for me. It's a lot of work, a lot of responsibility. It's quite hard, but very enjoyable. I am enjoying it.'

Steve has changed a lot in the last four years. At the start of Boyzone he was a home bird. He ached for his family and friends in Dublin when the Boyz left Ireland to go on to bigger things. When the world discovered the group, it took him away for long periods. He was painfully homesick, often reduced to tears. But that's all changed. He has grown into his role in Boyzone and has learned to enjoy the lifestyle. He says, 'Going to South-East Asia, places like Bangkok, it's amazing to witness the culture there at first hand and see what the people are about. We have been out there several times now and we're getting to know them a bit better. I also love Australia – beautiful people, beautiful weather, sunshine all year round. I could live in Australia. I could actually live there.

'I do sample the local cuisine when I'm in different countries. We've been to places like Argentina, Brazil and Chile and the food there is just wonderful. Spicy foods, I like that kind of stuff. I am adventurous where food is concerned, but only to a point. I wouldn't try all of it. I only sample stuff with ingredients that I know. I wouldn't taste squid or octopus. Shane would. Shane would taste anything.

'Travelling opens up your mind to a lot of things. You're getting to see the world, the good and the bad side of it. There's a lot of poverty out there as well. A lot of poverty in those countries. It's quite sad when you go down a street and see people with no legs sitting on the sidewalk, begging for money. That makes you really appreciate what you have in life.

We've been blessed with good fortune. It hurts to see other people getting a raw deal in life. It's terrible to see them suffering.'

Steve will never have to worry about money for the rest of his life. Boyzone's worldwide success has put him in the millionaire bracket. It takes years for the cash to filter back to the stars. But it's coming in and Steve's financial worries are a thing of the past. Money isn't his god, though. Steve is not materialistic or flashy. He doesn't flaunt his wealth. 'The only thing that would mean a lot to me is a house of my own,' he says. 'Somewhere I can go and say, "This is mine." You can't enter here unless I say so. I'd like that. It's a kind of protection for me. My own private little place away from the rest of the world. A place where I can be at ease with myself. That's all I want. I haven't bought one yet because life in Boyzone is so hectic. When it's all over, that's what I'd like to do. It's probably the only big thing that I'll splash out on.

'I'm not the type of person who would go around spending too much money on myself. I'm not a selfish person. I love spending money on other people. I love treating other people. I love treating my family all the time. I always make sure that they are OK. I try to help other people. I find that more satisfying than buying things for myself. I don't really place much value on material possessions.'

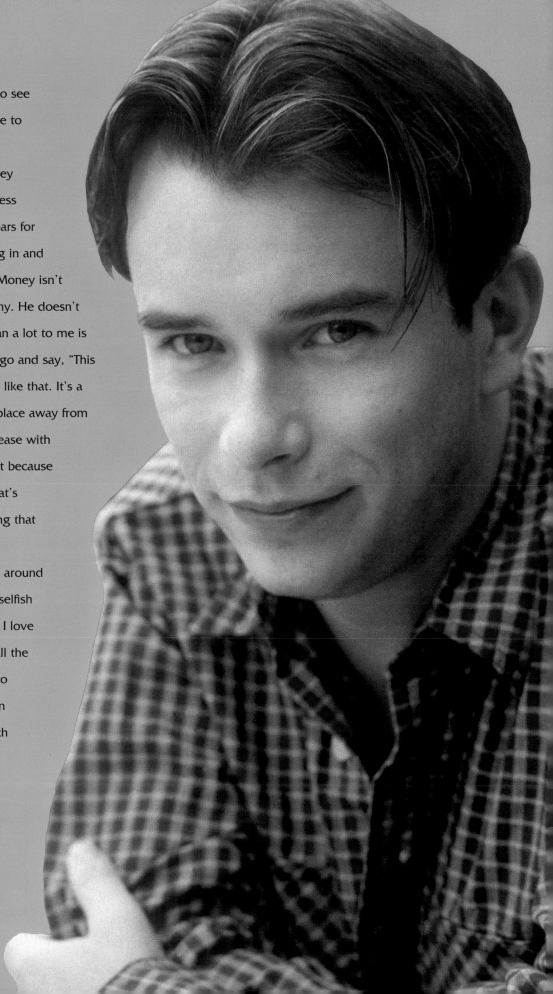

THE SHOW

A video scene announces the shock news that five famous young men are lost in space.

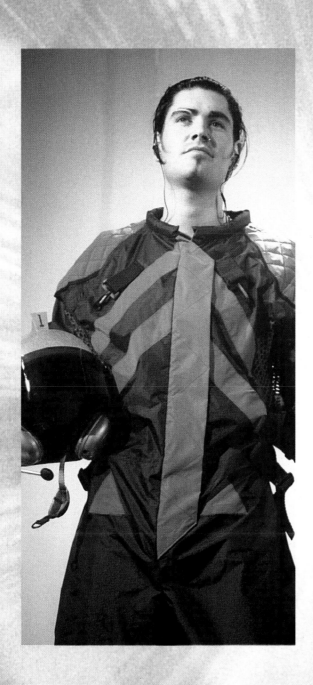

To deafening screams, thunderous applause and the shrill of ear-piercing whistles, five spacemen appear out of the cosmos on another planet. That planet is the stage. The missing five are Boyzone. It's the summer of 1997 and they are about to unleash the biggest show of their career.

This is the live extravaganza the Boyz always dreamed of being in a position to give their fans. After four years of hard work, they finally have the financial clout to afford it. The 'Different Beat' show costs over £500,000 to stage and it takes five massive trucks to transport it from venue to venue. Ronan Keating is adamant that this is just the start of Boyzone's mega-shows. 'This is the show we fought for,' he says. 'It's been a long time coming, but we got here eventually. It's about bloody time we got here, I have to say. Now we want it bigger again after seeing this. It's wonderful ... it's a mountain ... it's a fantastic show.'

There was a lot of behind-the-scenes work involved in creating this sound and vision masterpiece. Months of preparation involving the entire team behind Boyzone, as well as the Boyz themselves, eventually produced the finished show that was finally unveiled for the first time in Scotland's Aberdeen. Choreographer Melinda McKenna reveals: 'We had meetings to discuss ideas. We'd bash them around in our heads and we came up with – first of all – the space scene. I wanted to try to get something into video form at the beginning of the show that would really make the fans go mad. So we started off with the space theme. Then we

wanted to go back in time to the Groucho Club, which was a
1920s nightclub, and in the same vein we wanted to take
that into future nightclubs which was the seventies' disco
medley. And then the last section of the show is Boyzone
as they are.

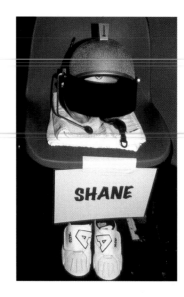

'We introduced eight dancers into the show. They
were brought in to give another energy and another look.
Basically we now don't have to rely on technical things.
We can still have people performing on stage when the
Boyz are getting changed. It's really important to have a
show that flows and that's the brilliant thing about
dancers, they can keep a show flowing. It was the Boyz'
decision to have dancers on. We did Eurovision and the
MTV awards and that's when we really started to put
dancers into their big performances. Now the Boyz enjoy
having them on stage.

'The dancers don't overshadow the Boyz in any way. The dancers are there to help create a picture and certainly not to overshadow Boyzone, because the fans are there to see Boyzone.'

Melinda spent endless hours researching ideas for the live show. It's crammed with scenes from different eras and different time warps, although it doesn't follow a particular storyline. 'When we go to see shows we like to be taken on a little journey. Not just to go and see somebody and just sit there and listen to music or whatever, especially with Boyzone because they're a very visual band. We wanted to take people on a journey in this show, basically start in a scene and then go back in time and then end up as Boyzone are today.

'I had to fill my brain full of information to see if I could mould things and create a show out of it. I went to see every possible stage production in London's West End. I went to libraries, doing research on *Star Wars* and space suits and seeing every *Star Trek* and every science-fiction movie to try and stimulate something in my brain for an opening.

'I work very closely with the set designers. We have a really good team. Everybody sort of chips in, the lighting designer, everyone, for all the creative angles to Boyzone. I have always wanted to do a "captured in a jail" kind of thing with a video screen. Because of *Star Wars* being very popular at the moment, I tried to pick up on that and that's how the opening came about.

'I was always looking out for ideas for Boyzone. If I was sitting watching television I'd be looking and thinking, 'Oh that's a nice idea.' I just need images to stimulate my brain and to help me create ideas.'

For the Groucho Club scene, set in the 1920s, the dancers are at tables and the Boyz star as the cabaret act in white suits. 'We just wanted to change the look of the show completely and have something that people didn't expect to happen.

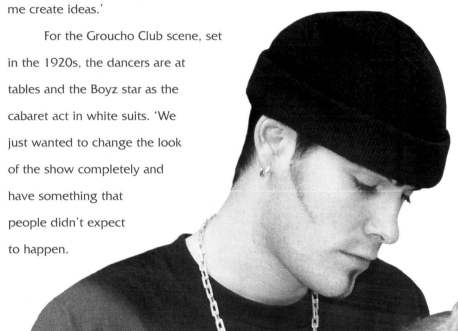

They are very classy in their moves. It's a real nightclub atmosphere with dancers sitting at the tables. We created a scene, rather than Boyzone just being on stage. There was a different feeling there. I watched quite a lot of the old movies to devise that.'

Then there is the seventies' nightclub scene, which is straight out of the movie *Saturday Night Fever*, complete with the medallion-man look. 'I love *Saturday Night Fever*,' Melinda admits. 'The whole big medallions around their necks thing, it was quite fun. We have never really approached that kind of fun side of things and I just thought it was something the Boyz could carry off without being too cheesy.

'The whole show is made up of sections that are pieced together. In the first section they've been captured. Then we take them back in time to the twenties and then on the seventies and then again to the nineties.'

There were high jinks going on during production rehearsals in the build-up to opening night in the Aberdeen Exhibition Centre. Allison Maund from *Boyzone* magazine was there on day one of the practice sessions and she captured the behind-the-scenes activities. How Melinda was having a hard time trying to round up the naughty five. Trying to get Steve down from a rigging ladder where he was swinging like a cheeky little monkey. How Ronan and Keith were running back and forward across the stage like out-of-control toddlers. Ro dancing and talking on his mobile phone at the same time. By early afternoon Ro is tired. 'Can I go to bed now? Me feet are about to drop off.' The answer is no. Steve and Ro performing a mini Boyzone version of *Swan Lake.* Ro doing his Liam from Oasis impressions. Shane singing into a Cherry Coke can. Mikey tucking into his croissant. And so on. Boys will be boys, but the work eventually gets done.

On show night, the Boyz usually arrive at the venue around 5 pm for a sound check and stay there until the show is over. Around 6 pm, it's time for dinner and they tuck in to the delicious food prepared by their own catering staff who travel with them. There are still a couple of hours to kill before they're due on stage. They relax by playing games like basketball. Shane messes around on his rollerblades. Keith winds up the crew. Mikey strums his guitar. Ronan listens to the latest CDs he's bought. Steve does his disappearing trick.

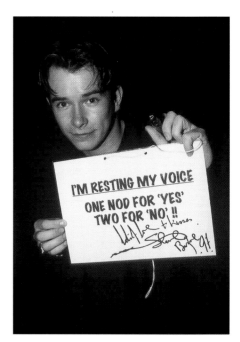

It's a real family atmosphere backstage. Before the show at Glasgow's SECC, the band and crew gather in the dining area where Steve Levitt the production guy is having his evening meal. It's his fortieth birthday and suddenly he's surrounded by people showering him with gifts of clothes and a magnificent watch before holding him down and spraying his hair with a red dye! A birthday cake is produced full of gooey cream and Steve decides to get his own back by digging out handfuls of cake and cream and lashing it at his attackers. Suddenly there's a ferocious cake fight with poor old Stephen Gately getting caught in the crossfire and ending up with blobs of cream all over him.

The Boyz usually meet competition winners before the show. In Glasgow, Amanda Cashmore and Jocelyn McBlain got the chance to be roadies for the day with Boyzone. Swoon! They were hanging out backstage with the guyz, chatting with them and getting autographs and photos. What a lucky pair! Amanda says, 'They're really down to earth. They're so nice, everything a fan would expect. They give lots of nice kisses and cuddles. They give you time. They don't just go, "Hi! Bye!," they stand and listen to what you have to say. They treat you with respect. I really appreciate them. I love them, I love them all.'

Jocelyn reveals: 'They're not just another boy band. I don't know what it is, but there is something different in their songs. Their music is more mature. I don't think of them as a teenybopper band because their songs are not just wee-bop-

along songs, they actually give you something to think about. You can relate it to your own life. It's really brilliant.

'When I first met them, I could not believe it was them in the flesh. Once I'd calmed down and realized they were real people, it was brilliant. I didn't scream in their faces because that would have scared them away. They were just people and it was really good to meet them. It was a brilliant day and I'll remember it for the rest of my life.'

The opening nights of the show in Aberdeen and Glasgow were spine-tingling occasions for the Boyz, who were so visibly proud of their mammoth production. As they scanned the sea of wide-eyed and open-mouthed fans in the concert venues, the Fab Five were left in no doubt that the show they'd created was a thriller. Two massive video screens on both sides of the stage come alive and a voice booms: 'Boyzone ... Origin: Planet Earth ... Status: Lost.'

Suddenly the venue in Glasgow erupts with a screaming mass of young fans. Five spacemen have made a dramatic entrance on stage and the Boyzone show has lift-off with the opening chords of 'Together'. The all-singing, all-dancing machine cranks up and powers through the opening numbers 'Strong Enough', 'Here To Eternity', 'Believe In Me' and 'So Good', and Shane inspects the fans to see if they've learned the Boyz' dance steps from the back of their *Live At Wembley* video. (Later he realizes it's on the *Said And Done* video, oops!)

Then it's time for Steve's special moment when he gets to be a solo performer, singing no less than two in a row, including his own song, 'Games Of Love' (accompanied by the energetic dancers). Steve enjoys it so much he doesn't want the song to end. 'Wow, it's over, that was fast,' he sighs.

Luckily, Steve has a second song, 'Don't Stop Looking For Love', which he dedicates to 'everybody here'. He's backed by singers Annette and Paulette, and the entire audience joins in as well. At the end the girls go wild when he flashes his cute smile and blows them a parting kiss.

There's a brief interlude, but you hardly notice because there's so much action on stage from the dazzling dancers. Then it's that voice again, announcing that Boyzone are back in the building as they swing into clubzone mode, in their white suits, black shirts and white ties, evoking gasps of astonishment from the girls in the jam-packed crowd. The excitement factor goes through the roof as they launch into their super fab hit song, 'Picture Of You', from the Mr Bean movie.

'Isn't It A Wonder' then precedes 'Love Me For A Reason', the song that started it all for the Boyz. Then Ro introduces the live musicians, Richard on keyboards, Guy on drums, Jerry and Tim on guitars and Annette and Paulette on backing vocals. The mums and dads in the audience love the next sequence because it takes them right back to the seventies with a medley that includes 'Night Fever', 'Blame It On The Boogie' and 'Stayin' Alive', with the Boyz trippin' the light fantastic, John Travolta style.

As the opening chords of 'Words' strike up, the manic crowd takes over the singing and Ronan acts as the conductor. There are video cameras at both sides of the stage capturing close-ups of the Boyz throughout the show, so the fans can see the facial expressions of their idols on the massive screens.

Ro next takes centre stage to sing the beautiful song 'Paradise' (which Steve introduces as 'one of my favourites') with the other Boyz on harmonies. After 'I'll Be There', it's time for the audience to take over the show again, singing the chart-topping hit, 'Father And Son'. Oh dear, it's getting perilously close to the end. Before launching into the final numbers, Ronan apologises to the fans for being out of the UK for a long time, explaining about their work in the Far East, Australia and South America. 'You stood by us. Only for you we wouldn't be on this stage tonight,' he acknowledges before the Boyz launch into 'What Can You Do'. They bring the curtain down with their big anthem 'A Different Beat', disappearing in revolving cones at the end. Minutes later they return for an encore and finish off the evening of sheer bliss with their Eurovision song, 'Let The Message Run Free', before disappearing again into the night, leaving deliriously happy fans in their wake.

After the show in Glasgow, Steve says, 'We really see tonight how things have grown since the first time we came here. Back then, we played in a smaller part of the venue and I remember it was on the same weekend East 17 were playing here. We were wondering would we ever make it to the big place. Now that we have done it a couple of times, it's amazing. A good feeling. A really, really good feeling. It's the fans that have done that, they've built us up and up and built us up more and more. So we say thanks to them.'

SHANE LYNCH

The tall, super-cool-looking young man struts up Dublin's fashionable Grafton Street, attracting admiring and curious glances from the afternoon shoppers milling along the pedestrian walkway.

He's oblivious to the mayhem he is creating all around him. At least, he gives the impression that he doesn't notice all the attention being paid to him. He's not the least self-conscious. He's the Mr Cool Of Pop. It seems that nothing could faze him. Nothing that rattles his cage will send him into a fluster.

If there's one individual who stands out among the 'five ordinary lads from the north side of Dublin', it's Shane Lynch. Everything about the boy screams Star. He's got the look. The image is perfect for a pop icon. The style is distinctively street cred. The hairstyle and little tufts of facial hair are unique. The studs that protrude from various parts of his body are in keeping with someone who is leading a showbiz lifestyle. The gold chains dangling around his neck are flash. This is definitely Mr Pop. Mr Style.

Shane Lynch openly admits that style is hugely important in his life. He was always fashion conscious, but the boy wonder says he's more so now than ever before. 'Oh yeah, it's definitely more important at this stage,' he says. 'I think that's because in the beginning we didn't really have our own individuality or images. It was styled for us. None of us understood the business back then because we were all newcomers to the game. None of knew what path we wanted to take or what role to play in Boyzone.

'It was a learning process and I think at this stage of our careers we all know where we stand. Now we all know what we are good at and bad at. We all know our own individual personalities and styles, what we're into. I'm so different from the rest of them in a sense, like when anything is getting made for TV or whatever, I will not wear it unless it's baggy and that is that. And that's what it has come down to really. It's a good thing. It's me. It's not something that I've been told to do, it's just me. I'm very comfortable in clothes that are big and baggy and I love jewellery.'

Shane has always stood out from the rest of his pals in terms of his taste in fashion and the music that turns him on. 'I think all my life in general I've tried to be different from other

people,' he says. 'When I was about twelve I started to get into music. I didn't want to listen to the same music as everybody else listened to. So when I was that age, rap was a very hard thing to come by. You could get commercial rap, but not actually hardcore, the underground stuff that I wanted to listen to, so I had to import it. And when I started doing that, I think the whole style of black music influenced me in a certain way. I think it has actually dictated the way I walk and talk and dress. Not an awful lot of Irish people are into hardcore rap. There's a lot of commercial stuff, hardcore doesn't come into

it. You can get it in Ireland now, but you couldn't get it when I started to develop an interest in it. So that's mainly where my style and influences came from.

'I don't really know what it is about rap music that appeals to me. I think it's just a musical style that I like. I know Mikey can sit and listen to Eric Clapton all day long, whereas I wouldn't be able to listen to one of his songs. He just does not appeal to me. I don't really know why I became attracted to rap. I think its just what you are born with, what music you listen to within your family, growing up, whatever. I don't really know, rap just has a certain style, a certain attitude and a certain rhythm and beat that I really like. The message never came into it to be quite honest. I know most of the rappers sing about drugs, money, murder and things like that that are far removed from my background, but that never actually came into it.The lyrics ... I didn't hear the lyrics, I just heard rhythm and style.'

Although he was brought up a Catholic, Shane no longer practises that faith. He no longer considers himself to be a member of any organized religion. But he does believe in a God and says he has a spiritual side to him. 'I am spiritual,' he says. 'In a Catholic family, you go to church every Sunday. And like most kids, I didn't want to go to church on Sunday. I left school at fifteen and that's when I started making up my own mind. My parents kind of let me make my own mind up because I was getting older. Now, because of being around the world and seeing so many different ways of

living, the different ways people think, the Catholic religion doesn't appeal to me any more. No religion does. I believe in a God and that is it. After that, I don't practise any kind of organized religion. There's a God and I live my own way. And, basically, I'm happy living my own way, not hurting anybody, not interfering with anybody, just getting on with my own life.'

Shane has a background role in Boyzone. He's happy to be one of the Boyz. He doesn't strive to be a leader of the gang. He knows his weaknesses and his strengths. He stays within the areas tto which his talents are best suited. Shane is happy to let Ronan take the lead. 'Ronan progressed very well at the start. He got more confident than the rest of us, so therefore he wanted to do more than the rest of us. The rest of us shied away from the main spotlight and that's how he became Mr Public Eye. And to be quite honest, that's fine by me. He can have all the public eye stuff.

'Every day you read something about Ronan in the papers. Whether it's about this girl or that girl or whatever. He chose that role and he's happy with that and that's fine. In my case, I'm very happy in the background. I know my own role and I don't want to be Ronan Keating, me, I know exactly where I want to go.

'I think it often causes a lot of problems in groups when one person such as Ronan Keating takes the limelight. Other members of the group can't handle it and that's where the fighting comes in. The other members get jealous and that's why groups split up. If you know your own role, stick to it and don't worry about the guy out front. If he's doing a good job, then let him do it. That's what I'd tell any group starting out or having problems: just stick to your own role and don't try to be somebody you're not.'

Shane is not obsessed with fame. He's not desperately clinging on to pop stardom and has no burning ambition to be in the limelight for the rest of his life. Although he writes his own songs, he says he'll never release them. And when Boyzone's reign as kings of pop comes to an end, Shane intends to quit the business and slip out of the public eye. He says: 'I have a practical approach to my life in pop. I just live each day as it comes and try to enjoy it as much as I can. I don't make any plans to do this, that or the other. Whatever happens, happens, and that's how I deal with it. I'm pretty chilled out about it because it's a very fickle business. You don't know if it's going to be here tomorrow or not. So rather than getting very serious about it, I just take it in my stride. And if it's not here tomorrow, so be it.

'It will probably be one of the biggest experiences of my life. I know that. Being in Boyzone is just a crazy ride through life, man. It's fantastic, although it has its tough times, like any job. You do enjoy it and then there are times when you just hate it. But you take the good with the bad. We have a very good time, definitely ... it's an experience that none of us will ever ever forget. For the rest of my life, every time I'll think of something in the past, one or more members of the group will come into me head, so we're friends for life basically.

'There will be no life in the music business for me after Boyzone. I do write songs, but they're not for Boyzone and they'll never be released. They are for me. Just for me. The music that you're influenced by is the music that you will write. As I said, I'm into rap music, so therefore I am not a main writer in Boyzone. When I said earlier that I didn't listen to the lyrics in rap music, now when I'm writing it, it's all about lyrics. I write about what is going on in the world. If I'm there when Boyzone are writing songs, I will have my input, give whatever lines or harmony that come to my head and do my best.

'I know I won't write songs when the group is over. People ask me, "Do you write songs?" I do, but I often think the only reason I write them is so I can say, "I do." But they are for me and nothing else really. I wouldn't become a rap singer after Boyzone because I wouldn't insult the people in rap music by trying to do it. I know I couldn't do it as well as the true rappers, so I'm very happy just listening to it.'

Shane is enjoying his jet-setting days with Boyzone. He wants to experience the world now while other people are organizing his foreign travels. After Boyzone, he intends to lead a quiet life. 'Most definitely,' he says. 'I'm going to settle down and that is it. I'm not going to be a travelling man ever again. Maybe a two-week holiday like every Joe Soap. I know definitely what I'll do is race cars after Boyzone. The music business or the entertainment business or any kind of fame is not going to be there for me. Anything to do with the public eye such as TV or radio or that kind of malarkey, I'm not going to be interested in. Just me cars.

'Through my upbringing I've been to many foreign countries before Boyzone, so I'm able to adapt to other countries a lot easier than most of the Boyz. I take an interest in the different cultures because I know after the group I won't be

interested in travelling and having to do for myself what gets done for me. Like now, I just get on a plane and it takes me wherever I'm going and then at the other end there's someone to take me to a hotel. I don't have to organize flights or hotels, it's all done for me. So it's easy for me to see the world now. I wouldn't have the interest to organize all that for myself. So when Boyzone is over that'll be the end of me travels.'

Shane plans to go into hiding after Boyzone and he reckons Ireland is too small to disappear in. He'll be setting up a new home away from his native land. 'I certainly won't live in Ireland directly after Boyzone finishes because there's just nowhere to hide. When it's all over I'll want to become an ordinary person again and that means not having to face the public. That could never happen in Ireland, so I'll definitely be hiding outside the country.'

He gives the impression of being a very private person, a young star who guards his personal life. He doesn't discuss the people close to him. But he doesn't deliberately conceal the people in his life either. 'That's the funny thing, I'm far from very private,' he says. 'In fact, I'm so open that people don't even notice what goes on in my life. That's exactly what it is. Like, for instance, if Ro was seen with a girl, the reason why he's seen is because he's trying to stay low. He'll go to a fancy restaurant because he doesn't expect to see many people there who know who he is or whatever. That's why he gets noticed. I don't do that. I'll walk up Grafton Street in Dublin or Oxford Street in London with whatever woman I happen to be dating at the time. I am in your face so much, people don't even realize what's going on.'

Where relationships are concerned, Shane isn't the type who will kiss and tell. If the girls want to talk about it, that's fine. But he won't embarrass anyone by putting them in the

spotlight and talking about their intimate affairs. 'I don't have a problem in saying if I am or am not dating a girl,' he says. 'Personally, I feel it is up to the girl to say whether or not we're dating. It doesn't bother me if people know whether I'm dating or not. It's my life to that extent. I don't really care what people think or what they don't think or what they write in the papers. I know the way I live. I'm happy the way I live. To me, that's all that matters.'

Shane's easy-going temperament makes him the envy of all who know him. He's one of the happiest guys in the world. 'It's just the way I am,' he says. 'In interviews, I'm often asked what I do for relaxation. My relaxation is to go to sleep. I'm so relaxed all the time I don't need anything else. I'm sure my family and people close to me were concerned at the beginning that the success of Boyzone and all the work that involves would change me or affect me in some way. But it hasn't. I have developed as a person, yes, but that would have happened anyway because I was still growing up when I joined the group. I've grown up in the pop world and I've learnt to deal with it. And all I can say is that I'm a very, very happy guy.'

DREAM TEAM

Ireland's Mr Showbiz Louis Walsh is the guru who created the pop supergroup. He's the genius who heads up the Boyz' Dream Team, keeping their show running smoothly and their star shining around the globe.

Louis

Louis is the sixth member of Boyzone, their big daddy, a father figure they can turn to when problems arise. He's a fortysomething bundle of energy who lives, breathes and eats showbusiness: it's his life-blood. A man with a great sense of humour – an ingredient that's essential in the business – he's a fun guy to be around.

Boyzone has always been his dream, ever since he was a teenager growing up in the rural Irish town of Kiltimagh, Co. Mayo. After a colourful career as a manager to a host of Irish stars, including Eurovision Song Contest winners Johnny Logan and Linda Martin, Louis finally realized his personal fantasy. It may have taken him a staggering twenty years to achieve his ambition, but he got there in the end. The scale of Boyzone's success has left him gob-smacked. He never realized in his wildest dreams that they would be this big. But he's not complaining. It has even made him a pop icon to millions of Boyzone fans – he's mobbed by young girls on tour. A self-effacing chap, all the attention leaves him a little bemused and embarrassed. But he'll live with it!

Louis says, 'Boyzone was my dream. It's bigger and better than I ever thought. I thought I would have a big local act. Maybe a hit or two in England, minor hits. Maybe get *Top Of The Pops* once or twice. But it has exceeded all my expectations. They've done eight Wembleys so far. That's just incredible for a group that has come out of a small country like Ireland.

'I'm surprised at how far we have come. And I'm certainly proud of what we've achieved. We're the first pop group to make it big out of Ireland, so that has created a little bit of history. That's something that can never be taken away from us.'

Louis is a music lover and showbiz fan rather than a businessman. In the early days of the band, he selected their hits and fed the media with acres of Boyzone stories. Louis' greatest strength in the group is opening up new doors for the Boyz through the amazing network of people that he knows and cultivates, and dealing with the band's publicity.

He says, 'I work mainly with Ronan and it's so easy. He makes it all worthwhile. I like all the other guys a lot, but he is the whole thing for me. I absolutely love working with him. It's not like work, really.'

John Reynolds is the co-manager of Boyzone. He's the king of the Dublin nightclub scene where he runs the trendiest venues in town, the Chocolate Bar, the Pod and its sister, the Red Box. The Pod is frequented by the international stars when they're in town. And the Artist Formerly Known As Prince played one of his legendary secret club gigs there when he was in Dublin a couple of years ago. John is a man with the Midas touch and he looks after all Boyzone's merchandising business. Louis and John were friends and business associates long before the formation of Boyzone. And they became partners when John helped to finance the Boyz' first single.

Producer Ray Hedges has been the studio wizard behind their hit machine. Ray, who worked with Take That, co-writes with the Boyz and has been their main producer during the last four years. He has found them to be 'very exciting' to work with after discovering how they have brought their own distinctive style into their music and songwriting.

Their team on the road is headed up by Mark Plunkett, the tour manager. A former rock musician himself, Mark once played in a British band called the Little Angels. He's the Boss on tour, with overall responsibility for the day-to-day running of the massive operation.

Barrie Knight has the onerous task of looking after the personal security of the Boyz, while his partner Steve Alderton is in charge of tour security. They're also like big brothers to the Famous Five. Barrie says: 'It's a lot more than doing security. We tell the Boyz what they're doing for the day, how the day is going to go. And when they're feeling down we pick them up, basically. Steve does all the advance. He goes ahead and makes sure everything is sorted out before we get to our destination. I make sure they get in and out of the hotel and venue safely.

'We try to strike a balance between keeping the fans happy and the Boyz happy. It's hard. When they're staying in a hotel we do have hairy moments because there are always lots of fans around and it's hard trying to keep the situation under control.' Steve says: 'Usually I go ahead and try and get the Boyz booked in on the same floor of the hotel. And I ask the hotel, if possible, not to let any fans, groups of girls anyway, book in on the same floor. Fans do try to book in near the Boyz' rooms. Sometimes you'll get young girls with their parents, which isn't too bad because the parents are looking after the girls.'

'Some of the fans are really professional, with an amazing network, he adds. 'In Europe, they've got a network of friends from England who give them details of all our movements and when we arrive at airports the fans are there waiting. We discovered that one of their sources was working in an airline and she was passing on information from the details on the computer. 'What fans don't realize is that we're not just looking after the Boyz, we're looking after the safety of the girls as well. We go out in the crowd and watch the kids and that kind of thing.'

Melinda McKenna is the hot-shot choreographer who teamed up with the Boyz when they launched the group in Britain. A former dancer herself, Melinda has also worked with other artists, ranging from Bryan Adams and Mark Morrison to Louise and Ant & Dec. A native of Liverpool all her life, her grandad was Irish. Melinda says, 'The Boyz have a great mental approach to their shows. Their concerns for creating good shows has blown the socks off me. They're very, very

creative with me. They'll discuss ideas and how they can make them work for shows. They are very concerned about making good shows, so the fans can really enjoy them.

'They have really developed since I first started working with them. Their concentration, everything about them has completely changed. I no longer have to scream at them. Just give them a stern look and that's it.

'On the last tour I got the chance to work on a one to one with each member of the group. When you get five people together in a room, it's kind of, "Oh, he's doing better than I am," so it's a bit of extra pressure for them. One on one was a lot easier and I think that gave the guys an awful lot of confidence.

'I know with Keith, he used to stand and just look at me doing the moves and not actually do them himself. I helped him understand that he had to, when he saw me doing them, he

had to get it. In actual fact, Keith has got such a quick brain to pick things up. He has really, really worked so hard because he knew that he was behind. Out of everybody, I'm so thrilled at the way he has progressed, I really am. He actually didn't like going into dance rehearsals, but he really enjoys them now.

'I have allowed them to keep their personalities in the dancing. Their personalities are so brilliant that they should be allowed to come through and I think it's nice to see people go the wrong way occasionally, bump into somebody and have a laugh, that's what they are about. It shows that they are normal.'

The Boyz' stylist is Alex Delves and he's been around the world with the Fab Five, including the Far East, Australia and South America. He's the guy who kits them out for TV shows and public appearances. Alex says: 'I know what each one of them likes and what they don't like, so therefore, 'cos they don't have time to go and get it – that's what my job is. I'm a professional shopper. It's fantastic. I love spending someone else's money.

'Shane has his own very individual style. He's the one who is not the hardest to buy for because I know exactly what he likes. But he is the one who you have to think that little bit extra about before you buy. Ronan and Stephen have a similar taste, as do Keith and Mikey.

'They've all got their own individual style – the way they like to look and the way they like to dress. Shane likes really baggy clothes. Baggy trousers and big baggy tops. Keith likes tighter tops and straight-legged trousers. Ronan likes leather jackets and trousers that are not really tight or not really baggy. Same with Stephen and same with Mikey.

'They're not the type of band who wear exactly all the same clothes and all look really heavily styled. They're just five very individual blokes. They dress that way. Obviously there is some stuff, like for stage or TV, where they will all wear similar clothes or whatever. But for day-to-day stuff they don't like to look the same, like a lot of bands do. For their videos and stuff like that, they always wear what they'd wear normally. A lot of stuff I buy for them for TVs and videos, they wear day to day as well. It's just that they don't have time to go out shopping themselves.'

Boyzone's production manager Steve Levitt is an old hand at his job. He has worked with everyone from golden oldies Mick Jagger and George Harrison to young guns Ant & Dec and East 17. He teamed up with Boyzone when they did their first UK tour, even though they could barely afford him. His role involves organizing all the equipment, all the trucks and all the buses.

Steve says, 'When Boyzone started off it was very low key and we only had one truck. They were playing to a DAT machine because they didn't have any musicians. We slowly but surely progressed on to the next tour with two trucks and now we have five. On the first tour we had nine people in our crew, now we have fifty. Now their show is equal to anybody that has gone on tour at this level. There's nothing missing and there's more than most. The next tour will be bigger again. It increases by fifty per cent every time.'

Louis Parker is the agent who sells Boyzone's live shows to local promoters around the world. He also has acts like Peter Andre and the Prodigy on his books. Parker says: 'Boyzone have progressed from a very small pop act to being a major force in the pop industry throughout the world and

are growing at a phenomenal rate now. Boyzone's concert tickets in '97 has been the fastest selling on the pop scene and their merchandizing has now out-sold Take That in their heyday. Two to three million people will have seen Boyzone perform live in '97. And in '98 I would estimate five to six million will see them live because the gigs get bigger. Boyzone are the biggest selling boy pop band, and the most popular today.'

Sharon Dunne from PolyGram Ireland has travelled the world with the Boyz since she left school at the age of eighteen, looking after their press and promotion. It was Sharon's boss Paul Keogh who signed up Boyzone. 'It's been my full-time job, twenty-four hours a day sometimes, and a fantastic experience for me. They're a great bunch of guys, every one of them,' she says. 'I've seen them change, of course. Four years ago, Ronan was so shy – and look at him now, full of confidence. Shane was quiet, but now if he's got something to say, he'll say it. Stephen, Keith and Mikey haven't changed that much. They're easy to work with. Very professional when it comes to getting up and getting down and doing the interviews. After four years of it all, they haven't changed dramatically as far as I can see.'

Allison Maund is the important link between the Boyz and the fans. As the editor of Boyzone the official Boyzone magazine, she keeps the fans up to date on what happens behind the scenes in the Boyz' camp as they blaze a trail around the globe.

ALISON

Allison says: 'I was always a huge pop fan. I was a huge Take That fan. I'm a huge music fan, full stop. When I was in college, I worked in a HMV record store on Saturdays to earn some extra money. I used to be into A Ha. That was useful as well, because I used to think that Morten Harkett was the best man ever alive. And so, when I get letters from fans, I know what they're thinking and what they're feeling. I can still remember what it feels like.

'I qualified as a nurse, but never practised. I did a media course and I did some work experience with a publishing company in London and it snowballed from there. I did some freelance work, then I met somebody who was working with Boyzone's fan club and he knew about this magazine being set up and that they needed somebody to write it , so he put me in touch with the person concerned. I had seen the band. I'd been to the Smash Hits Poll-Winners' Party when Boyzone performed 'Love Me For A Reason' and won Best New Act on the road.

'Before the magazine launch, I was quite worried about the fact that I was a girl, working with these Boyz and writing for Boyzone fans who are primarily female. I was worried the fans might not like the fact that it was a girl writing for the magazine. But, in fact, I've had a brilliant response. I've had thousands of letters and not one of them has been bad. They see me as the connection between them and the band. They respond to articles that I write. Like one girl who wrote and said, 'I can just see Ronan taking the camera apart, like you said he did in Japan. Can you just tell him that I said he looks great.'

'I'd say I get at least 500 letters a week. I used to reply to every single letter. But now I hate the fact that it has got so big because I can't do that any more.'

Phil Ollerenshaw is the Boyz' official photographer. He previously worked with Take That on tour. He says, 'Boyzone immediately made me feel very at home. The minute I walked in the door it just felt like I had picked up where I'd left off with Take That. There are no similarities between Take That and Boyzone apart from the fact that both had five members.

'I have to be a fly on the wall photographing everything that the Boyz do. They're not at all worried about the picturesI take because they know and trust me now, as Take That did, not to take stupid pictures of them. I think you can take fun pictures without making them look stupid.'

PHILIP

KEITH DUFFY

It's seven o'clock in the morning as Keith Duffy slips off to bed at a posh hotel in Glasgow, having entertained the Boyzone road crew all night long.

He'll catch a few hours of shut-eye before emerging early for a quick shopping spree in the city. Keith is the number one 'party animal' in the group, enjoying every moment of his life as a pop star on tour. And he's got a seemingly endless supply of energy. While the rest of the gang collapse around him, Keith can whoop it up all night long.

The burly lad loves entertaining people with his cheeky wit, general good humour and high jinks. One night back at a hotel after the show, he sparked off a peanut fight! He grabbed a handful of peanuts from a tray and lashed them at Mikey and a group of dancers sitting around an opposite table. Suddenly there was war, and everyone in the bar was being showered with salted peanuts. Keith laughed his head off. Someday, he says, he'll grow up!

Keith is a kid at heart. And he loves the company of people. He's probably the most sociable member of Boyzone, a big teddy-bear character who's always game for a laugh. You'll never find him sitting around waiting for something to happen. He's the guy who will be creating the action, coming up with the fun ideas to make daily life interesting. To the outside world, Keith is a jolly young man who doesn't appear to have a care in the world. But there's a darker side to him that is rarely revealed.

He says, 'I hate being on my own. I get very lonely on my own. It's not that I dislike my own company. It's just that I'm quite a deep type of person and if I'm given too much time alone I think about things that don't need to be thought about and I get myself upset. I prefer being in the company of other people all the time. I just love being around people. I'm a people person. So that involves being a bit of a party animal. It's not that I'm crazy or touched in any way, I just love socializing.'

So much has changed in Keith's life since Boyzone was first launched on to the pop scene. He's now a superstar who has travelled widely and is idolized by his fans. And he has earned the kind of money that other people can only dream of. But, fortunately, he hasn't been affected by it all. He says, 'I know the image people have of Boyzone, they think that we're massive and something special. But the reality is, we're just ordinary people, and I have never lost sight of that. I just love being myself. You get such a kick out of being ordinary in this business. It's so easy to be star-struck and have people do everything for you, it's so easy to do that.

'It's not easy to stay on the same level. So, it's actually a buzz to stay on the same level. People are so funny. You get a great laugh off other people when they realize that you're only an ordinary bloke having a laugh, making mistakes like everybody else. When you see the realization on their faces, it's just a buzz, better fun than playing at being a star.

'I think that one of the secrets of Boyzone's success is that the fans can actually relate to the people we are. You see groups that dress to kill, they are in the gym every day and they have a certain style, people copy their style. Boyzone have

never been any of that. We are five ordinary boy-next-door blokes.'

With the incredible success that Boyzone has achieved, the money has been rolling in. The five young men are now in the millionaire league. It's a mind-blowing fact that can also be difficult to handle at such a young age. Keith admits he's not obsessed with wealth but he likes splashing out on whatever takes his fancy. He says, 'Obviously I have a few quid. But I spend a lot of money. Money doesn't mean anything to me. Now I can have all the things that I would have liked to have had years ago, so I just go and buy them. I often pop into a department store to have a look around and I usually end up buying some item. I'd buy something like a pair of sunglasses, even though I've got a pair the exact same at home. I don't even need them. That's me.

'I don't let money run my life. I'm having too much fun to do that. I know too many nice people and they're more important to me than money. I was always happy-go-lucky without money. All right, it's made me a little bit more confident in certain situations having a few quid, but it's definitely not the be-all and end-all of everything.'

Keith is tall, handsome and powerfully built. He has a great personality and a friendly smile. He's easy to like when you get to know him, a joy to be around, and he makes new friends easily. His personable nature is one of his biggest attributes. But despite this, Keith admits he lacked confidence in himself before finding success with Boyzone. Before he became famous, he

compensated for what he considered to be his lack of charisma by concentrating on his physical appearance to gain attention.

He says, 'Before Boyzone I was in great shape. I was body building and had a really good body. But I had no confidence in myself, none whatsoever. My sole confidence was in my body. I used to wear a little string vest going to nightclubs and girls would say, "You have a great body." It even impressed the blokes. They'd ask, "How long have you been working out, man?" All that positive attention made me feel good about myself.

'That's the only confidence I had, but it was false confidence. Then I had a car crash with Shane and did me back in and me shoulder and I couldn't train for some time and a lot of the muscle turned to fat. I was a big fella anyway, so I ended up looking fat and plump and that left me feeling really down. But now I'm starting to get myself in really good shape again. Not really, really good, just real good.

'But making a success of your life also helps to build your confidence and self-respect. I've met so many nice people since starting this life with Boyzone. I can go up to people who know who I am now and talk to them and I don't feel anyway embarrassed about talking to them. I talk to them eye to eye. Now I don't care. I know I'm a nice guy, I know I've got a big heart, I know I can do a lot for other people and I know I've got a lot of good mates around me who understand me. So I've no problem

communicating anymore. I've no problem making friends.'

It's difficult for the boys to juggle their personal lives and high-rolling career with Boyzone. They often have to go on stage with a smile on their faces, even though they may be be cracking up inside because of personal traumas. It happened to Keith earlier this year. He says: 'I went through a really low period in my life this year. There were things in my personal life that I had to deal with and it was a very emotionally trying time for me. I hit rock bottom. I mean rock bottom, really rock bottom. I was stressed out. I felt as though I was forty years of age for a while, I really did. I felt so old and I'm not getting into that state any more. I'm relaxed now. I'm calm. If I'm depressed I mind my own business. You'll never see me not laughing. I'm always smiling and laughing. Nobody will ever know what I'm going through. It's nobody else's business and to be honest with you, nobody wants to listen to you moaning. They can pretend to be a really good friend and care, but at the end of the day you've got the problems and you have to deal with them. It's all right getting someone's opinion, but you're better off just trying to sort it out yourself.

'I was close to breaking point, but I got through it. I channelled everything into Boyzone and it got me through it. We started touring and through the work I got all the negative things out of my system. Now I can honestly say I haven't been happier. I've never been more

confident. I've looked better, but I've never been more confident and I've never been happier, so I'm on the right road again. That's why I can enjoy this business a hell of a lot more than I could in the past, because there were too many things not letting me enjoy it. But now I see it from a whole new perspective. I know how to do the job in the way that I'm not overdoing certain things and not underdoing certain things. I have a happy medium. I'm having a ball, a great time. I don't mind the work. I love going out smiling and laughing and making everybody laugh. It just comes natural to me. People might laugh at me, but I don't care – that's all part of the fun.'

Conversation flows fluently from Keith these days. He doesn't struggle to find the right words. There are no embarrassing periods of silence. He speaks with an air of confidence and a certain amount of authority. While he admits he was always a 'talker', his vocabulary has expanded and his world travels and work in Boyzone have given him a varied range of experiences to talk about.

'I was always a bit of a blabber-mouth,' he says. 'But I do admit that my old dictionary in the head wasn't the best at times. I didn't know that many long words. I know marmalade and all now. I was never afraid to talk up for myself. I used to always say what people were thinking. Other people might agree with you when you speak out, but they wouldn't have the confidence to say it and they wouldn't have the guts to say it. My big mouth got me into trouble a lot at first when we first started. I'd go into a meeting with all

management and record company and say exactly what the other Boyz were thinking. But I was often left on my own. It took the Boyz a while before they would say, "We're with you." So I shut up for a while because there was no point putting myself out when nobody else was. All the lads in

Boyzone are very well spoken now, everybody can hold their own and do a proper interview.

'Through the interviews I have done, and the things I've done, the experiences I've been through in the band and in my private life, it's made me a much broader-minded person. I can adapt to a situation a hell of lot quicker than I could have years ago. I won't jump at something when I'm annoyed, I'll just put everything in proportion. The best way to handle situations is to be relaxed about them and talk them out in a reasonable manner. I don't raise my voice. I don't get into fights. I don't get into rows with people. If people are hot-headed, I walk away. It might upset them at the time, but when they cool down they'll understand why I've done it. I don't fight with no one, not my parents, brothers, mates, anybody. If anybody raises their voice to me, I'd rather walk away and talk to them when they're relaxed.'

Keith once shaved his head because he was being hassled by guys in Dublin after he joined Boyzone. He felt the skinhead look gave him a tougher image. 'Guys were giving me a hard time, calling me "queer" because I was in a boy

band. So I had my head shaved because I wanted to feel a little bit intimidating. I wanted to be a bit different, feel like a lad again, not in a boy group, so I shaved my head and people were afraid for their life of me. When I went into the chipper at nightime, there was never one remark. It was a good laugh. I looked terrible, though. The fans and all were totally intimidated by me. I just didn't look well at all. I didn't feel good about myself at all at the time. But that's all changed and I let my hair grow again.'

Through tours with Boyzone, Keith has now become a man of the world. The band has taken him outside Dublin and introduced Keith to places and people in faraway destinations. He has now become accustomed to other cultures and it has made him more adventurous. Boyzone has been his university for life. He has learned more in the last few years through his global travels than he would ever have done had he remained at school and completed his formal education. He's been lucky – and he knows it.

He says, 'Boyzone has opened my eyes. It has taken me outside Ireland and shown me what a big world it is out there. What a wonderful world it is. I have seen so much in a short space of time. But there's lots more I would like to see and experience. There are so many interesting things I'd like to do and so many places I'd like to live. I'd like to learn more about other cultures. I'm definitely more broad-minded now. The Far East is an amazing place. It's totally different. Every culture is different out there. I like Asia a lot. It's a great experience. South America is fantastic and I love Australia. They're all places I never expected to ever visit. It's been just amazing. I hope it continues. I don't want this to stop. I'm having too good a time. It beats working for a living.'

ON THE ROAD

The Boyz arrive in Bangkok and, discovering that they have a few hours of free time, there's a stampede to the local markets.

It's humid, noisy and crowded, with people scurrying in all directions. But it's a wonderland for the Fab Five as they scan the rows and rows of market stalls. They've found an Aladdin's Cave and, with almost every item under the sun available at bargain prices, they while away a couple of fun-packed hours sifting through the enormous variety of goods.

Bangkok is Bootleg City and it has superb copies of all the latest CDs, designer gear and branded products ... just as good as the real thing and dead cheap! Hours later, a chirpy gang of Boyz arrive back at their hotel and traipse up to their rooms on the seventeenth floor, laden down with bags of goodies. They're still buzzing with the excitement of their afternoon adventure and are all geared up for some devilment. With some more time to kill, it's the ideal chance to have harmless fun with the laser pens that Keith and Shane have just bought. Down on the street – seventeen floors below – the unsuspecting folk of Bangkok are going about their daily business. Suddenly, it looks as though they're being attacked by an alien force. It's the Boyz flashing laser shards down on the street in front of the locals, stopping them in their tracks. There's a man with a red spot on his forehead, wondering why he's attracting the attention of passers-by. A dog yelps with fright when the flash of light appears in front of him.

The Boyz collapse in fits of laughter. Isn't it a wonder they're not locked up! But such childish pranks help to keep them sane as they grapple with the demands of life as pop stars. They have a good sense of fun, camaraderie and curiosity when they're touring around the world. Touring beats sitting in their rooms getting bored and watching TV, something they could easily do at home. Even the local taxi service in Bangkok provided an entertaining game for the Boyz. The taxis or *tuk-tuks* are two-seater carriers which are drawn by small motorbikes. The Boyz and other members of their crew hopped into several of them and convinced the drivers to have a *tuk-tuk* race. The locals, who enjoy driving at high speed anyway, were happy to oblige. There the popsters were, whizzing along narrow streets at the speed of light, screaming their heads off and letting off steam. A dangerous bit of fun, but it's good to play.

Keith Duffy took time out to decorate his body with yet another tattoo when he went under the needle of top

Bangkok artist Jimmy Wong. It took Keith two hours to decide what tattoo to have done – and another four hours to have the job carried out. Keith, who was very brave throughout the entire operation, had a massive Celtic cross inscribed on his upper arm, covering an old tattoo. In February in Hong Kong, Shane also made a trip to the tattoo parlour for some more body artwork. 'I got two more tattoos on my chest,' he revealed. 'I already had one that said "unity" in Chinese, so I got another two to go with it.

They spell "truth" and "friendship". It wasn't sore and it didn't take very long.' Stephen left Hong Kong with an armful of gifts from the local fans. 'I got lots of Calvin Klein underwear and aftershave and tons of Disney stuff.'

In Japan, Ro thought Tokyo was like Batman's Gotham City with its enormous buildings. After interviews, the Boyz went exploring and (surprise, surprise) shopping, with Ro and Steve treating themselves to fantastic mini disc players. 'I think Japan has got the best shops I've ever

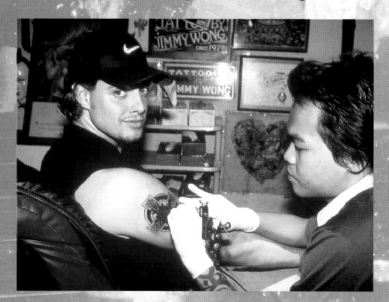

seen,' Ronan says. 'It's really expensive, but that doesn't really matter because the fans give you so many presents – CD players and everything.' There was a night out bowling in Tokyo with some lucky prizewinners and then they all took part in the ancient Japanese custom of … karaoke!

They also got the chance to sample the local cuisine in the very up-market restaurant of the Tokyo Hilton after their appearance on the local *Mega Pop Kiss* TV show. The delicious fare was cooked in front of them and it was all very civilized until madcap Keith Duffy decides to liven up the proceedings by egging on the band's bass player Paul to sample a very, very hot mustard-type thing. It's so hot you can't taste any more than a tiny piece the size of a finger nail. Keith offered Paul lots of money to eat a spoonful. The cash was placed on the table and Paul fulfilled the bet. Then another member of the group said, 'I'll give you another £100 if you eat the whole lot.' Silly old Paul duly obliged and ended up really, really ill. He was drinking pints of water for hours afterwards. Paul was a lot richer at the end of the night, but he admits it didn't make up for the pain. Duffster strikes again!

The best part of being in Boyzone for Keith is when he's on tour. There's a great party atmosphere in the Boyzone camp. Keith and the Boyz enjoy the feedback they get from the fans on stage, and they're buzzing with excitement for a couple of hours after each show, so they have a laugh together before retiring to bed. Keith says: 'Although there is a little bit of promotion to do from time to time, most of the day is spent just touring around, meeting a lot of interesting people, having a good time and making new friends. Then at the end of the day you go on stage and you think that's the icing on the cake, but there's more icing after that when you go back to the hotel, its just a big mad party then.

'When I'm away I don't sit in my hotel room. I'll go to a restaurant for a meal and a laugh, or go out with the record company, or go out with the promoter. I'd go out with anybody who wants to go out and I'll just have a laugh. A lot of the time the boys will come too. Some boys will go one night, some boys will go another night, but I go *every* night.'

In the early days of Boyzone Keith was a gym fanatic. Any spare moment he could find in his busy schedule, Keith would use the time to work out to hone his muscular physique.

running to stay in shape and keep up his stamina. Keith says, 'I don't do an awful lot of weights anymore. I do more exercising. I run four to six miles every day because it sweats all the toxins out of your system, then I do some stretching exercises after the run. The only body parts I exercise are my chest, my shoulders and I do a bit of work on my stomach from time to time. I would like to have a small waist and big shoulders, but I'm not into the Peter Andre-style built-up muscle. I think girls can relax with you a lot easier, or people in general can relax with you if you're not perfect. They can relate to you. I have more of a manly body than a bodybuilders' body.'

In Brazil, the Boyz, with the exception of Steve, were thrilled when they were invited to visit the pits and garages at the Interlagus Circuit during the Brazilian Grand Prix. Steve has no interest in cars and can't even drive. But the rest of the guyz are car fanatics and motorbike freaks. They got the chance to check out the Ferraris and even touched Damon Hill's car. Legendary British motor-racing commentator Murray Walker, who organized the tour with

UK TV personality Andi Peters of *The Noise*, said: 'You've been able to do something today that very few people get to do, to get into the pits and garages and talk to the people. There are millions of people around the world who would give their eye-teeth to be where we are right now.'

Afterwards, Mikey told Andi, 'This was just an unbelievable day for me. Before I came in to Boyzone I worked as a mechanic for almost six years, so this was something special.'

In March the Boyz visited Rio and the Corcovado Statue, a major tourist attraction. Andi Peters succeeded in embarrassing poor old Ro by producing two cuddly toys the Boyzone star takes with him on tour, a tiger called Treggs and his little brother, Tristen. Ro's brother, Gary, who was on holiday with the Boyz, had smuggled the little furry animals out of his bedroom. 'This is so embarrassing. I'll kill Gary when I get him,' laughed Ronan.

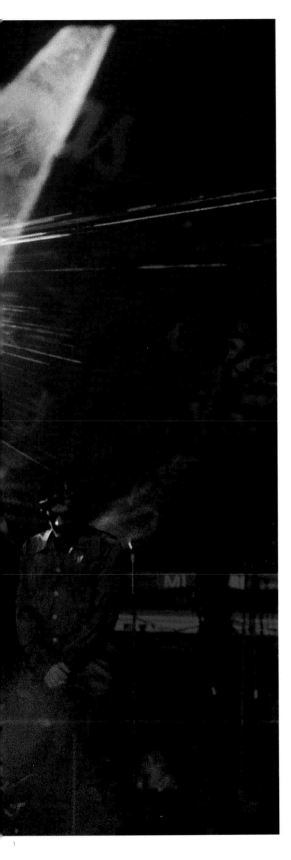

The Boyz always visit the local Hard Rock Cafés when they're on their foreign travels and pick up mementoes of their visits to exotic cities. Keith reveals: 'We collect these glasses called hurricane glasses. They're used for a cocktail, the Hard Rock Hurricane, which is a rum-based cocktail. It's lethal, it would blow the head off you. But the glasses are beautifully shaped with the Hard Rock logo on them. Underneath, each glass has the name of the place where you drank the cocktail, like London, Tokyo, Bangkok or Sydney. From Europe to Asia to America they have these glasses and if you finish the drink you get to keep the glass. We've been collecting the glasses all over the place. I think we've about sixteen now. That's one thing we do to remind us one day of having been to those places.'

They're back in the UK on tour and Boyzone's big white bus has left the venue after another sellout show. The Boyz, dancers and band are all aboard. Suddenly, Shane's nose starts to twitch. He sniffs again. Someone on the bus has lit up a cigarette. 'Please announce that this is a no-smoking bus,' he politely asks the driver. The offending person down the back – not one of the other Boyz – immediately stubbs out

his ciggie. The Boy is happy. If there's one thing that gets up Shane's nose, it's smoking. Despite this minor incident, there's a great atmosphere on the tour. Phil the photographer says, 'It's a real family feeling. There's a nice big bus on this tour so everyone travels together – the five boys, eight dancers and five musicians and it's dead good; it's like being in a big gang.'

If there's one member of the group who keeps the stage performance under close scrutiny it's Shane. 'I'm very involved with the show. I take a lot of pride in it. I help Melinda every now and then because dancing and choreography is my thing. If I think something should be there, or shouldn't be there, I'll say it. We're not professional dancers, but we have a certain standard on stage. We can't do flat-out dance routines either because we have to sing. You have to have a happy medium and I

suppose that's where I get involved, just try to keep that happy medium.

'I like everything in the show to be very slick. I get pretty annoyed when things don't go right and someone is not doing something they're supposed to be doing, even the slightest arm movement. If I actually catch them not doing it, that gets me pretty annoyed. I know I'm not perfect myself, sometimes I don't do it, but that's for one of the other boys to tell me. I've always got something to tell someone after a show.'

Being in a band is like being a member of a family. Eventually individuals get on each other's nerves and it leads to little tantrums and flare-ups. With Boyzone, it's been the same. They've always got on well as a group, but occasionally during the course of their career there have been differences between individuals. Four years on, having soldiered on together in all kinds of situations around the world, they've never been closer. Keith says, 'We've got on so well for the last year. We've always got on well, but from

time to time we might have had little tiffs along the road, just kind of figuring out who we were. But right now, we're just best buddies. We understand each other. The boys understand me so well, it's scary.'

During a couple of days off from touring in June, the Boyz had a special 'bonding' evening in their native city of Dublin. Instead of going out to an expensive restaurant, they decided to buy some beers and have Chinese takeaway food at an impromptu party in a local public park on the north side of the city where they come from. Steve remembers, 'The five of us and some of our mates decided to go drinking in St Anne's Park, which is in a place called Raheny. We got a takeaway from a Chinese restaurant called Wong's, which is just around the corner from the park. We were there for about four hours, just hanging out and having a laugh. We were standing, sitting down, playing football, having great fun. Nobody bothered us. None of the fans spotted us, so it was a really private time for us. We caught up on old times and got back to reality. We sat down and talked about the experiences we've had over the years, what we've done in the last four years, stuff like that. It has brought us a lot closer. The five us have been brilliant since. We'll have to do that again. We arrived in the park about 8 pm and after midnight we went on to a local nightclub together.'

Their schedule is always busy and varied. Shortly after their new show was launched on the live circuit around the UK, the Boyz were filling in days off with additional projects like the Mr Bean video for their hit, 'Picture Of You'. That was a fun day for the guyz when they teamed up with the hilarious Rowan Atkinson, alias

Mr Bean. With Mr Bean on the scene there was bound to be an accident and, right on cue, Mikey accidentally struck Ronan in the face, giving poor old Ro a bloody nose. It wasn't serious and the action continued after a pause for Ro to recover. Ronan says, 'Working with Rowan Atkinson was a fantastic experience. There was no script, he just made it up as he went along, all the movements, everything. The guy is a genius because he makes it look so easy and natural. His facial expressions are a killer. We wet ourselves laughing.

'If you look at that video for 'Picture Of You' you'll see a resemblance to the one we made in the Australian outback for 'Isn't It A Wonder'. With Mr Bean involved we decided to do a send up of that one, so instead of the big Cadillac and Harley Davidson bike, there's a little three-wheel van and a scooter!'

Two days into the UK tour, Keith is in trouble. Outside the Hilton Hotel in Glasgow a large crowd of fans are staging a vigil where Boyzone are staying. It's early afternoon and Keith decides to go shopping alone. The taxi goes to the back of the hotel to pick him up, but the fans suss what's going on. As Keith leaves the rear exit he spots the frenzied gang of girls stampeding towards him. He dives into the taxi, landing on the floor. The girls swarm around it and start to thrash the car all over. Inside, Keith is scared. And the taxi driver is not impressed. Fortunately, the hotel security staff arrive on the scene and get the fans under control. Keith says, 'I should have had our own security with me, but I didn't. I'm a big bloke and can look after myself better than the other guys in the band. But I got murdered because there were too many of them [fans]. There's nothing you can do when there's too many of them. You can't see them directly one on one, so they know you're not going to see them and you're not going to dislike them if they do something to you, so they'll pull your hair or pull your earring out or something, just to have it. And that's what happened in Glasgow.

'Barrie [the Boyz' security bloke] was supposed to ring me and say when he was going to town and I was going to go with him, but he never rang me. I wanted to go to town shopping, so I rang Steve [the Boyz' other security chief] and I couldn't get Steve. So I rang Mark [the tour manager] and said I was going to town and I'd be grand, no problem.'

In the centre of Glasgow, Keith had to contend with hordes of young girls as he tried to shop. But this time he had the situation under control. 'It took me about an hour to walk five minutes because there were so many fans around,' he said. 'I was just breezing through them no problem, no rushing, taking my time, I was saying, "Relax, sit back, I can't see what I'm doing." Making them all relax, taking it easy, just getting through to them that I wanted to do a bit of shopping. That I've been in town for an hour and bought nothing, give me five minutes and I'll meet you on the way back down. I said, "Please don't follow me, I want

to go shopping." So eventually they said "No problem, Keith." I went and did my business and I came back and they were there. And everything was cool.

'I'd be lying if I said I don't get tired of it sometimes. I don't get tired of the fans, I get tired of not having my privacy sometimes. But I don't raise my voice. I don't get stressed out anymore, so it's very easy to be good to fans when you don't get stressed out. I wake up in great form. I wake up and I can't wait to get out of bed.'

Later that evening, as Boyzone are boarding their coach on their way to the performance, there are about 100 young girls outside the Hilton. This time, Barrie is in control. He organizes an orderly line and the Boyz get off the bus to sign autographs for them. 'Fans, where would you be without them? Where would we be without them? They have put us where we are. They are the life of Boyzone really. They are the life,' Steve says on the way to the gig. 'I know sometimes we're tired, but when you do go out to them, they do appreciate it. Sometimes it's quite difficult because there are so many girls and it can get out of control. They start ripping your clothes and tearing them. It's not only our safety that we have to worry about, but their safety as well. There might be smaller kids there who could get hurt and you don't want that to happen. That's why we have to have security to keep things under control, but we do pay a lot of attention to our fans. You have to respect them. You can never take them for granted. They are who we are; they make us what we are.

'I would just like to say a big thanks to them because they are fantastic. I am always answering letters. Last night at the show there were two letters addressed to me. I answered back. If there are letters in there with stamped addressed envelopes, I will write back to them. All they want is an autograph. I'm happy to do that if it's going to make some kid smile.'

Ronan sits on a private plane as the Boyz are whisked to their next round of promotions. He's reflecting on his incredible position in the pop world. Ronan has come a long, long way in four years. A naive teenager now transformed into a handsome, mature and experienced pop idol with the world at his feet. Right now Boyzone are kings

of pop. But they're keeping a grip on reality. Ronan sums it up: 'What we're doing is trying to create our own road. We're trying to be the best we can be. But you never know what's around the corner. It's a very fickle business. People forget you very quickly. Look what happened to Take That.

'I was on stage last night and I said to myself, "I want this to last forever." The thought of not doing this kills me. I know it won't last, we all do, so we're going to enjoy every moment of it while it's still rolling along. Being in Boyzone is the trip of a lifetime. Nothing will ever compare to it.'